# Arthritis Pain ...
## Heal Arthritis Natu
### I Did, You Can, Too!

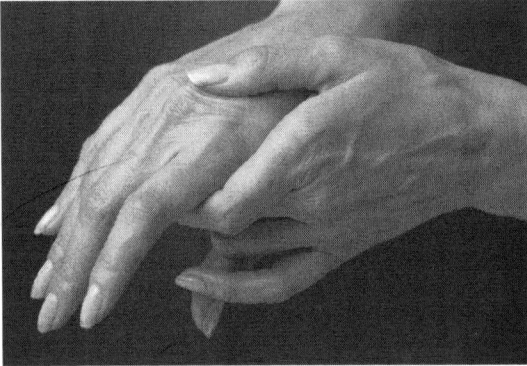

**MARLENE SHIPLE, Ph.D.**
**THE LIFE COACH DR.**
**http://thelifecoachdr.com/coach**

# Arthritis Pain ... *FREE!*:
## Heal Arthritis Naturally –
## I Did, You Can, Too!

# DEDICATION

To all of those who have had a part in the healing journey that I undertook – to Pat Godfrey, who first introduced me to the concept and work of Edgar Cayce; to Gereaux Boutrous, who suggested hair analysis as a medical pathway to cause; to David Patton, who made the inspired suggestion that I use Edgar Cayce's findings myself!

To all my family and friends, without whose encouragement I would not have had the endurance and courage to continue my healing search.  To my brother Fred, on whom I can always count for caring support.

To my cadre of learned editors and gifted readers – Moira Lynn, Glenn Medici, Denise Pelletti, and Kathy Rose – who helped me breathe engaging readability & delightful vitality into this manuscript!

AND

To you, who grace me with your desire to read these words … You are the very reason that this account was written. Each one of you is the reason for this book coming to be!

# FORWARD

I have written this book to share Hope with those who deal with the misery and suffering of Arthritis. I was there ... I completely KNOW what you are going through. If you ever wished you could find someone who understands each iota of what you are experiencing each and every day – day in and day out – let me hasten to assure you, I UNDERSTAND!

Thirty years ago, I was led to an incredible, miraculous solution. This solution was a treasured find! The healing that I experienced as a result of this solution has endured throughout the interim – and left me pain-free – and Arthritis-free – for the past 30 years!

Let me be quick to make clear: I do not have super-special healing powers. I am an ordinary human, just as you are. What I did was find an effective healing process – a combination of steps that I used over and over – steps that I continued to invest with energy and persistence and confidence – and did not give up on – until it worked! I've written this book to lay out these steps ... to share them with you. I do so in the belief that you, too, will get to see how well they can work for you!

My Message is simple:
Here are the specific healing steps that worked for me.
This remedy has continued to work for 30+ years!
 It took me 14 years to perfect the working formula
  … to discover what worked
  … and eliminate what DIDN'T.
I absolutely do NOT think that it will take you that long:
I've crystallized the specific steps that created Success!
They proved effective for me – I encourage you to use
  them -- To discover for yourself how they work for you!

# Arthritis Pain ... *FREE!*:
## Heal Arthritis Naturally –
## I Did, You Can, Too!

# Arthritis Pain … *FREE!*: Heal Arthritis Naturally – I Did, You Can, Too!

# PART I:  MY EXPERIENCE
## Chapter 1:  The Depths

Pain.
Aching ... incessant ... joints full of misery, crying out.

Stiffness ... making it difficult to even want to get up and move.

Pain ... so intense... When you do begin to move, it leaves you incredibly sorry you thought to do so.

Yet, you cannot just stay sit there, lie there ... the constant aching throbs and builds ...

If you just lie there, in pain, the misery seems to intensify ... until it threatens to consume you.  It builds in intensity until you think you just can't stand it another moment ... but you do, you have to.

What choice do you have?

There is nowhere you can go to evade it.  It is inside you -- you carry it with you, as though it were a part of the very fiber of your being.

Pain with each pulse beat ... painful throbbing that reverberates in synchrony with each beat of your heart.

So, you decide to get up and walk around -- to do something, anything!  You think it to yourself, "It's going to hurt anyway, and so I might as well do something.  At the very least, maybe I'll feel productive."

You rationalize to yourself that you might as well feel good about getting something done. Perhaps, the feelings of accomplishment will be a distraction from the pain.

Sometimes, it is ... for a brief while. And, then, the pain reassumes its position of dominant superiority.

Since your feet hurt more when the weight of the body presses them down, this additional pain inevitably "wins" out. You want to cry out ... but that would accomplish nothing. "Just keep walking," you tell yourself, "maybe the ongoing motion will allow the aching to wane ... a little."

Pain in the toes and feet, in the ankles, in the knees. Hot stabbing pain in the hips, in the shoulders, in the neck, in the jaw. Thick throbbing in the elbows, in the wrists, in the fingers. Both sides ... intense, unrelenting ...

This is the Face of Arthritis.

For 14 years, from 1966 to 1980, this saga of pain was my constant companion. It filled my days with misery. It brought intense fatigue and weakness. It resulted in feelings of despondency and helplessness. And, despite the massive energy drain, it awakened me at night ... at that bewitching hour -- 2:00 - 4:00 a.m.

Night after night after night ... no matter what time I fell asleep ... I would awaken ... then, because of the intense pain, I would find myself unable to fall back asleep again. Sleep deprivation left me bone-tired, energy- drained, and totally hopeless to know how to get the repeated cycle to end.

It was the constant, persistent, unrelenting backdrop to my other activities. For, through it all, I kept pushing to remain active, productive, and alive. I felt that I HAD to maintain quality of life, I HAD to experience spirit and joy and passion … in the everyday – amazing – commonplace mysteries and miracles of life!

So, during these 14 years, I continued to live …

I started my university studies in Ohio. During my fourth semester there – my last in Ohio – I became seriously ill. The Miami River Valley was experiencing almost-constant rain that season; the humidity was intense. I reacted to all of that rain and humidity with intensified the pain, stiffness, and infirmity. Then, I contracted a serious case of the flu.

I seemed unable to shake the disease and recover. My body started to swell up … I didn't know why. Worst yet, the doctors that I consulted did not know why. At that time, quite simply, I thought I was going to die – I couldn't move and I was getting worse. I was scared.

Once I completed that semester, I quit school and stayed with my parents. I knew I had to do something. I was miserable, in constant pain, and still swelling up more and more. I didn't know what to do – I just knew I had to do something – something had to change!

During this time, my father related a conversation he had had with a business associate. This man lived in Phoenix, Arizona, part of each year. He described how much better he felt physically – how much more he could do – when he was in the drier climate of Phoenix. This sparked my thinking … could Phoenix be a solution for me?

I hated the thought of leaving my parents, and my family and friends, and everything familiar in my life. It was the hardest thing I had ever done to that time. Yet, I was so ill that I feared I would not be able to create a viable life unless I found relief for my physical health. In a word, I was desperate!

So, at the age of 22, I got flight reservations, packed up my belongings, and moved 2,000 miles across country. Let me be clear about this: This was 2,000 miles away from everyone and everything that had ever provided me with comfort – to a city where I
knew no one – driven to find a drier climate – in the hope that this would equate to reduced infirmity and pain. What great motivators pain and infirmity can be!

One ironic, funny addendum to this story …

On the flight to Phoenix, I had struck up a conversation with the woman seated next to me. She had resided in Phoenix for a number of years; she was returning home.

I had told her that I was moving to Phoenix for the dry climate and sunshine. Of course, when we landed in Phoenix, it was in the midst of a pouring rainstorm. I'm sure I looked somewhat forlorn because she rushed to reassure me, "Oh, my dear! How regrettable – it's raining … and you came here for the sunshine. It really is USUALLY sunny here."

I'm pleased to report that the move did accomplish sufficient decreases in stiffness and pain that I was able to start to function again. Determined not to dwell on the huge emotional cost, I started in – got a job, made new friends, developed new social affiliations, and soon returned, once again, to college.

I worked full-time during the summers and part-time while attending university during the school year. I went to innumerable medical appointments – truly, a "career" in and of itself! I studied, completed assignments, passed examinations, earned a Bachelor of Science degree; and then, later, earned a Master of Science degree. I opened my own business – providing coaching and counseling services to clients.

I visited family, socialized with friends –old and new, dated, traveled around the country, and vacationed at different times in several European cities. With careful attention to having adequate strength, I completed household and yard-work tasks. I read, cooked, rested, baked, and attended a multitude more doctors' appointments. I actively engaged in daily exercise.

I learned to pace my activities so as to maximize my energy. I became an expert in the art of recharging and re-energizing through the use of frequent naps. I learned how to do high-energy-demanding tasks when my energy was highest. I meditated and used self-hypnosis routinely. I prayed regularly, and kept my spirituality alive.

This – ever so briefly – describes my activities during these years.

And, always, I was coping with steady, throbbing -- frequently, stabbing -- pain. Just the constant nature of the pain was wearing; dealing with it, exhausting. Because of the constant pain, physical tasks became more demanding. Mental tasks – like those required for memory, studying, and learning comprehension – were also made much more demanding.

Ironically, an added stressor was caused by the fact that I did not LOOK like I was seriously impaired. When you have a broken leg, people expect you to need to rest more, use crutches, get extra help, etc. When your illness is invisible – as mine was – it misleads people into thinking you are well … and "should" be acting like a well person – "You don't LOOK sick.". The "invisible illness" leads to a greater sense of confusion and lack-of-understanding regarding the actual condition. And I couldn't fault others for this – I looked just fine: How could they ever comprehend the intensity and constancy and depth of pain that was going on inside me?

Then, there was the depression ...

Chronic pain brings along with it an overwhelming sense of hopelessness and helplessness and desperation. These feelings typical of severe depression are common for a person suffering from chronic pain. You absolutely KNOW what you have lost ... there is a new reality to experience. At the same time, it feels like something you have never faced before, something brand new that you have never been taught, never been prepared in any way, to face.

It feels that way, specifically, because it is something you have never faced – or been prepared to face – before!

Having never faced it before, you have not built resources -- effective resources – to support you to know how to effectively deal with this level of pain or infirmity or inflammation or physical weakness or stiffness or joint-disfigurement.  Not knowing what to do or how to do it ... dealing with constant, unrelenting pain ... feeling exhausted and fatigued all of the time ... not sleeping well ... not knowing what can make it better …  Not knowing what to try. Not knowing what not to try.  All of this has a combined effect of sending the chronic pain sufferer into the depths of emotional despair.

Or, at least, it did me ...

The Good News for me was that emotional despair was far from my usual state of being.  By and large, I have always been an optimistic person.  Life worked well for me to be that way!  By being optimistic – and reaping positive outcomes of being so – my very optimism had been reinforced and strengthened by my life experiences.

[Now, in case it is not normal for you to be optimistic, I'd like you to invite you to consider changing this.  Developing a more-positive manner of thinking is a matter of learning something new.  I heartily recommend it!  Later in this book, I'll be more specific about why this is so important. However, even if – in the past – you have not been an optimistic person and even if you choose not to change that now, the methods that I describe in this book can still work beautifully for you!]

In my life, I built on that tendency toward optimism by using purposeful positive thought, meditation and other spiritual practices.  The result of this was that I received a boost over the negative, depressing aspects of my condition.  By staying busy – actively engaged in learning and growing – interacting in helpful ways with others – I could put my mind on higher good … and away from immediate misery.  I took FULL ADVANTAGE of doing so whenever – and for as long as – I could!

Yet, in the meantime, during my many years of living with this disease, there were the drugs ...

They were all prescribed for illness-related purposes;  e.g., to manage pain, to reduce inflammation, to deal with side effects – to enable me to survive and keep going.  Not that the medication eliminated the pain, taking enough to do that would have rendered me completely incapable of any activity – or coherent thought – whatsoever.  The meds merely sufficed to take-the-edge-off the pain ... and create even-more bone-wearying fatigue.

Dealing with all of this was a trial.  At times, I was not pleasant to be around -- I would snap irritably, be blatantly unreasonable, or be forced to cancel plans at the last minute because I quite simply just felt too badly to be able to get out of bed.   Having it happen once was disappointing; having it happen repeatedly was irritating – not only for me, but also for anyone else who had planned to go with me.

At the end of that 14-year period of dealing with Arthritis, I was taking 24 aspirin each day, I was on daily prednisone (oral cortisone), and I received an injection of gold salts every 10 days.  I had been on almost-every research drug being investigated at that time (My rheumatologist participated in research studies aimed at finding better treatment approaches for Arthritis.). Over time, I took drugs with names like Placidyl, Percodan, Lasix, Darvon compound, Decadron, Indocin, Phenaphen #3, Valium, Bellargal, Lomotil, Compazine caps, Diazide caps, Prednisone, Motrin, Soma, Plaquinil Sulfate, Naprocin, and Cytomel. I also – intermittently – received Cortisone with Celestone injections. Yikes!

Each time a new drug was introduced to my regimen, I'd feel such incredible hope: Maybe this would be the one ... ? Maybe, this time I would have the medication that would bring such-sought-after relief – or, possibly, a cure! I'd take it diligently ... and look – expectantly – for even the slightest sign of improvement.

I'd carefully watch and move each joint -- looking for reduced swelling, less redness and heat, more limberness, lowered stiffness, reduction in aching, improved sleep, even-a-little-less pain. Each time, I would – again – face the disappointing truth: This one didn't work either.

And my spirits would plummet ... again. It was grim.

*No passion so effectually robs the mind*

*of all its power of acting*

*and reasoning as fear.*

-- Edmund Burke

# PART I: MY EXPERIENCE
## Chapter 2: The Hope

Yet -- despite all reason -- during this whole time, I maintained an over-riding optimism that being afflicted with Arthritis would NOT be my lifelong experience. I nurtured a belief -- sometimes, bright, sometimes flagging, sometimes, so dim as to be almost-invisible -- that, someday, I would find a healing solution to remedy this affliction.

I had an over-riding sense of knowing that there was a cure. Even though I saw people who had suffered from Arthritis for decades, I had a knowing sense that there was something that could stop and reverse it. Furthermore, I sensed that, if I were diligent enough – if I turned over enough rocks and continued to research possibilities – I could be successful in finding what I needed to overcome it.

I was relentless. I researched. I repeatedly plagued my Rheumatologist with questions. I exhausted avenue after avenue. I was scrupulous and diligent in trying out each possibility. I followed each protocol to the letter.

If something came to my attention – from copper bracelets to acupuncture to gin-soaked raisins to salt under the tongue – I gave it a try. I felt that, if I didn't at least give it a test, I'd never know how my body would uniquely respond to it.

I incubated a "knowing" that there was a cure for – a remedy to – all of this misery. And I was determined to try anything-and-everything that came to my attention in order to find that solution ... that I just knew -- intuitively -- existed!

And, one blessed day, I found it!

In the last section of this book, I will share with you the journey that left me in the delightful condition of being Arthritis Pain … *FREE!* This quest turned out to be so successful that it kept me both pain- and disease-free for the past 30 years!

# SECTION I : MY EXPERIENCE
## Chapter 3: The Promise

So, perhaps, you have been asking yourself, "Why have you kept quiet all this time?" "Why have you kept this to yourself?"

Actually, I haven't kept it to myself. I've shared this solution with many people over the years ... and I have been delighted to witness these other persons enjoy similar results to those I'd experienced myself!

At the same time, I did NOT want to give anyone false hope. I wanted to be absolutely certain that what I have experienced for all of these years was a result that others could create for themselves, too. I wanted to know WHY it worked ... so I could thoroughly explain the workings to others.

I have strong integrity. I was cautious not to offer people a solution that would not perform for them. I was unwilling to make promises that were false -- that would not produce desired results! To me, that would have been not only immoral, but also cruel. Remember -- I was the person who had searched so relentlessly ... and been severely disappointed time after time after time after time.

I was absolutely unwilling to subject another person to that same disappointment.

Over the last 30 years, I have learned more about why what worked for me, worked as amazingly -- miraculously -- as it did! Over the last 30 years, I have become more versed in what healing is ... and the forces that make it work!

This understanding has brought me full-circle to the Truth: Universal Principles – Universal Laws – work ... each and

every time! The creative function of the subconscious mind works ... each and every time! Scientific findings and Brain Science give us explanation about why this works ... each and every time! All we need do to experience our own miracle is apply the Universal Principles, the subconscious-mind creativity, the Scientific findings and the Brain Science research-results purposefully – with understanding and diligence, with certainty and persistence!

So, here is my Caveat and my Promise:

The Caveat: No half measures! Please read this book in its entirety. Before you think about undertaking this solution for yourself, understand fully what is required. Please take the time to understand why this system works ... and why it can work for you?

Then, if you choose to undertake to create a healing solution for yourself, be ready to follow each step ... every day ... for the full time-duration that it takes. Be willing to commit to yourself ... and not stop short of total success! By doing so, you open up the channels that allow success to be YOURS!!

The Promise: Oops! I couldn't restrain myself ... I just gave you the Promise! Here it is again: Success can be YOURS, too, if you are diligent in using this complete system!!

# Arthritis Pain … *FREE!*:
# Heal Arthritis Naturally – I Did, You Can, Too!

PART II: ARTHRITIS

SECTION I: THE DISEASE
  Chapter 1: Scope of Arthritis
      Chapter 2: Prevalent Types of Arthritis
          -- Osteoarthritis
          -- Gout
          -- Systemic Lupus Erythematosus
          -- Fibromyalgia
          -- Rheumatoid Arthritis

SECTION II: DEALING WITH ARTHRITIS
  Chapter 1: Management
  Chapter 2: Medical Consultation
  Chapter 3: Risk Factors
  Chapter 4: Physical Activity
  Chapter 5: Pain
  Chapter 6: Insomnia
  Chapter 7: Social Support

**Arthritis Pain … *FREE!*:**
**Heal Arthritis Naturally – I Did, You Can, Too!**

PART II: ARTHRITIS

SECTION I: THE DISEASE
  Chapter 1: Scope of Arthritis
      Chapter 2: Prevalent Types of Arthritis
          -- Osteoarthritis
          -- Gout
          -- Systemic Lupus Erythematosus
          -- Fibromyalgia
          -- Rheumatoid Arthritis

# SECTION I: ARTHRITIS: THE DISEASE
## Chapter 1: Scope of Arthritis
## Nation's Most Common Cause of Disability

**ARTHRITIS: What Is It?**

While the word *Arthritis* is used by clinicians to specify joint inflammation, it is used in public health to refer more generally to more than 100 rheumatic diseases and conditions that affect joints, the tissues that surround the joint and other connective tissues. The pattern, severity, and location of symptoms can vary depending on the specific form of the disease.

The most common arthritic condition is Osteoarthritis. Other frequently occurring forms of Arthritis include Rheumatoid Arthritis, Gout, Lupus, and Fibromyalgia.

Typically, rheumatic conditions are characterized by pain, stiffness, and swelling in or around one or more joints. The symptoms can develop gradually or suddenly. Some forms of Arthritis – such as Rheumatoid Arthritis and Lupus – can involve the immune system and affect multiple organs and cause widespread symptoms.

Although Osteoarthritis is more common among adults aged 65 years or older, people of all ages (including children) can be affected. Nearly two-thirds of people with Arthritis are younger than age 65. Arthritis is more common among women (24.4%) than men (18.1%) in every age group, and it affects members of all racial and ethnic groups.

## Extent of Arthritis:  Public Health Problem?

### High Prevalence

According to the Centers for Disease Control & Prevention (CDC), an estimated 46 million U.S. adults (about 1 in 5) report doctor-diagnosed Arthritis.  This makes Arthritis the nation's most common cause of disability.  In addition, a recent study indicated that some form of Arthritis or other rheumatic condition affects 1 in every 250 children.  Arthritis continues to be a large and growing public health problem.

As the U.S. population ages, these numbers are expected to increase sharply.  The number of adults with doctor-diagnosed Arthritis is projected to increase to 67 million by 2030, according to the study published in the January 2008 issue of Arthritis & Rheumatism.  More than one-third of these adults will have limited activity as a result of this increase.

"The prevalence of arthritis overall continues to grow in the United States, which is not surprising given that many of the specific conditions are age related and the general population is aging," said Charles G. Helmick, MD, a CDC epidemiologist and a lead author on the study. "The increases in some of the more common types of arthritis suggest that they will have a growing impact on the health care and public health systems and more efforts should be made to promote underused but effective interventions and programs that could reduce that impact," he said.

## Common Disability

Arthritis is the nation's most common cause of disability. Nearly 19 million U.S. adults report activity limitations because of Arthritis each year. Among all U.S. adults of working age (18–64 years), about 1 in 20 reports that they have Arthritis that limits their work. Among the 23 million adults with Arthritis in this age group, Arthritis-attributable work limitations affect about 1 in 3 people.

## High Lifetime Risk

A recent community study estimated that the lifetime risk of developing knee Osteoarthritis serious enough to cause painful symptoms is 45%. Risk increases to 57% among people with a past knee injury. Lifetime risk for knee Osteoarthritis affects 3 in 5 people who are obese and also goes up with increased weight.

## High Costs

In 2003, the total cost of Arthritis was $128 billion, including $81 billion in direct costs (medical) and $47 billion in indirect costs (lost earnings). This total is equal to 1.2% of the 2003 U.S. gross domestic product. Each year, Arthritis results in 992,100 hospitalizations and 44 million outpatient visits.

## Risky Complications

Arthritis makes it more difficult for people to be physically active, and not being physically active is a risk factor for many chronic diseases. More than half of adults with diabetes or heart disease also have Arthritis. Research shows that pain, fear of pain, fear of worsening symptoms or damaging joints, and lack of information on how to exercise safely prevent people with Arthritis from being physically active. To manage chronic conditions such as diabetes, heart disease, and obesity effectively, people with Arthritis need help finding ways to overcome Arthritis-specific barriers to physical activity.

# SECTION I: ARTHRITIS : THE DISEASE
## Chapter 2: Prevalent Types of Arthritis

There are five types of arthritis that are most common. These include Osteoarthritis, Gout, Systemic Lupus Erythematosus, Fibromyalgia, and Rheumatoid Arthritis. I'm going to briefly describe each of these Arthritic conditions, before going into more detail about Rheumatoid Arthritis.

I. **Osteoarthritis** is a disease characterized by degeneration of cartilage and its underlying bone within a joint, as well as bony overgrowth. The breakdown of these tissues eventually leads to pain and joint stiffness. The joints most commonly affected are the knees, hips, hands, and spine. Its specific causes are unknown. Disease onset is gradual and usually begins after the age of 40.

Treatment for OA focuses on relieving symptoms and improving function. It can include patient education, physical therapy, weight control, and use of medications.

II. **Gout** is a chronic rheumatic disease resulting from deposition of uric acid crystals (monosodium urate) in tissues and fluids within the body, a condition known as hyperuricemia. This process is caused by an overproduction or under excretion of uric acid. Certain common medications, alcohol, and dietary foods are known to be contributory factors.

Acute gout will typically manifest itself as an acutely red, hot, and swollen joint with excruciating pain. These acute gouty flare-ups respond well to treatment with oral anti-inflammatory medicines and may be prevented with medication and diet changes. Recurrent bouts of acute gout can lead to a degenerative form of chronic Arthritis called Gouty Arthritis.

III. **Systemic Lupus Erythematosus** (SLE/Lupus) is an autoimmune disease in which the immune system produces antibodies to cells within the body leading to widespread inflammation and tissue damage. The exact causes of SLE are unknown; they are believed to be linked to genetic, environmental, and hormonal factors.

SLE may be characterized by periods of illness and remissions. SLE has a variety of clinical manifestations and can affect joints, skin, brain, lungs, kidneys, and blood vessels. People with SLE may experience fatigue, pain or swelling in joints, skin rashes, ulcers, seizures, and fevers. A team approach in treating lupus is often warranted due to the number of organ systems involved.

IV. **Fibromyalgia** is a syndrome predominately characterized widespread pain, abnormal pain processing, sleep disturbance, fatigue, problems with thinking and memory, and, often, psychological distress. The causes of fibromyalgia are unknown; however researchers hypothesize that genetics and physical and emotional stressors are possible contributory factors to the development of the illness.

There are difficulties in diagnosing fibromyalgia, since its clinical picture can overlap other illnesses and there are no definitive diagnostic tests. Multidisciplinary treatment is recommended, including screening and treatment for depression. Patient education, pharmacologic agents, and other nonpharmacologic therapies are used to treat fibromyalgia. Exercise and anti-depressant therapy have been shown to be effective to improve outcomes for people with fibromyalgia.

V. **Rheumatoid Arthritis** is a systemic inflammatory disease that manifests itself in multiple joints of the body. The inflammatory process primarily affects the lining of the joints (synovial membrane), but can also affect other organs. The inflamed synovium leads to erosions of the cartilage and bone and, sometimes, to joint deformity. Pain, swelling, and redness are common joint manifestations.
Although the definitive causes are unknown, RA is believed to be the result of a faulty immune response.

RA can begin at any age and is associated with fatigue and prolonged stiffness after rest. There is no cure for RA, but new drugs are increasingly available to treat the disease. In addition to medications and surgery, good self-management, including exercise, are known to reduce pain and disability.

A. **Background**

* Rheumatoid Arthritis (RA), an autoimmune condition, is a chronic inflammatory polyarthritis. (1)

* Natural history studies of RA suggests that RA follows one of three courses
  * Monocyclic in 20% of people initially diagnosed with RA (i.e., had one episode which abated within two years of initial presentation and did not reoccur).
  * Polycyclic in 70% (i.e., fluctuating levels of disease activity).
  * Progressive and unremitting condition in 10%. (3)

Another natural history study found that 75% of people with RA experienced remission after five years. (4)

* Historically, pharmacologic treatment of RA has traditionally followed the pyramid approach. That is, treatment starts with corticosteroids/non-steroidal anti-inflammatory drugs, and then progresses to disease-modifying anti-rheumatic drugs (DMARD) and finally to biologic response modifiers (BRM) if persons are non-responsive to the previous drugs. Today, a more aggressive treatment approach is being advocated for people with early RA, with prescription of DMARDs within three months of diagnosis. (1)

* Diagnosis
  * The 1987 Am College of Rheumatology criteria are used in the clinical diagnosis of RA, and to define RA in epidemiologic studies. Persons must meet four of seven ACR criteria; (5) these criteria are based on clinical observation (e.g., number of joints affected), laboratory tests (e.g., positive rheumatoid factor), and radiographic examination (e.g., X-rays evidence of joint erosion). (5)

* Early RA is typically defined as RA that is diagnosed within 6 months of symptom onset. There is extensive interest in early diagnosis of RA because early treatment may improve disease prognosis. The only U.S. study to examine time between symptom onset and diagnosis reported a median lag time of approximately 4 weeks between symptom onset and medical encounter, and a median time of 18 weeks between medical encounter and RA diagnosis (A total median lag time of 36 weeks) (6). These authors noted that there was even a delay in diagnosing patients with most identifiable features of RA (e.g., morning stiffness and seropositive rheumatoid factor), and concluded that early disease recognition is challenging as only half of those who eventually develop RA initially present with features specific to the condition.

* Risk factors
    * A range of environmental and genetic variables have been evaluated as potential risk factors for RA (e.g. hormonal exposures, tobacco use, dietary components, HLA genotype, and microbial exposures), but to date no definitive risk factors for RA have been identified.
    * Of the environmental factors examined, the most consistent evidence exists for an association between tobacco use and RA; most studies of this risk factor have found a history of smoking is associated with RA onset with increased risks ranging from 1.3 to 2.4. (2)
    * The role of the following four estrogenic factors in RA etiology has been studied extensively:

§**Oral contraceptives (OC)** — Early studies found a decreased risk of RA among women who had ever used OCs, a relationship that has not been confirmed in recent studies. (8–10)

§ **Hormone replacement therapy (HRT)** — There is mixed evidence of an association between HRT and RA onset. (9–10)

§ **Live birth history** — Most studies have found that women who have never had a live birth have a slight to moderately increased risk of RA. (10)

§**Breastfeeding** — The most recent studies have found that RA is less common among women who breastfeed; this is in contrast with earlier studies which found an increased risk associated with breastfeeding. (10)

*Genetic susceptibility markers. Most attention has been given to the DR4 and DRB1 molecules of the major histocompatability complex HLA class II genes. The strongest associations have been found between RA and the DRB10401 and DRB10404 alleles. (2)


B. **Prevalence**

* An estimated 1.293 million adults aged 18 and older (0.6%) had RA in 2005, down from the previous 1990 estimate of 2.1 million. (11) This is partly due to a more restrictive definition of RA, but in part reflects well-established declines in RA prevalence around the world.

* The prevalence among women in 1995 was approximately double that in men (1.06% versus 0.61%). (11)

* This study observed almost a 2:1 ratio in prevalence for women to men (1,367 per 100,000 (95% CI=1,175-1,558) among women compared with 736 per 100,000 (95% CI=561-912) in men.) (7)

## References:

1. Guidelines for the management of rheumatoid arthritis: 2002 Update. *Arthritis Rheum* 2002;46(2):328–346.
2. Silman A. Rheumatoid arthritis. In: Silman A, Hochberg MC, editors. *Epidemiology of the Rheumatic Diseases*. Oxford University Press, 2001;31–71.
3. Masi AT, Maldonado-Cocco JA, Kaplan SB, Feigenbaum SL, Chandler RW. Prospective study of the early course of rheumatoid arthritis in young adults: comparison of patients with and without rheumatoid factor positivity at entry and identification of variables correlating with outcome. *Semin Arthritis Rheum* 1976;4(4):299–326.
4. Pincus T, Callahan LF. What is the natural history of rheumatoid arthritis? *Rheum Dis Clin North Am* 1993;19(1):123–151.
5. Arnett FC, Edworthy SM, Bloch DA, McShane DJ, Fries JF, Cooper NS et al. The American Rheumatism Association 1987 revised criteria for the classification of rheumatoid arthritis. *Arthritis Rheum* 1988;31(3):315–324.
6. Chan KW, Felson DT, Yood RA, Walker AM. The lag time between onset of symptoms and diagnosis of rheumatoid arthritis. *Arthritis Rheum* 1994;37(6):814–820.
7. Gabriel SE, Crowson CS, O'Fallon WM. The epidemiology of rheumatoid arthritis in Rochester, Minnesota, 1955-1985. *Arthritis Rheum* 1999;42(3):415–420.

## References (cont'd):

8. Brennan P, Bankhead C, Silman A, Symmons D. Oral contraceptives and rheumatoid arthritis: results from a primary care-based incident case-control study. *Semin Arthritis Rheum* 1997;26(6):817–823.

9. Doran MF, Crowson CS, O'Fallon WM, Gabriel SE. The effect of oral contraceptives and estrogen replacement therapy on the risk of rheumatoid arthritis: a population based study. *J Rheumatol* 2004;31(2):207–213.

10. Karlson EW, Mandl LA, Hankinson SE, Grodstein F. Do breast-feeding and other reproductive factors influence future risk of rheumatoid arthritis? Results from the Nurses' Health Study. *Arthritis Rheum* 2004;50(11):3458–3467.

11. Helmick CG, Felson DT, Lawrence RC, Gabriel S, Hirsch R, , Kwoh CK, Liang MH, Maradit Kremers H, Mayes MD, Merkel PA, Pillemer SR, Reveille JD, and Stone JH for the National Arthritis Data Workgroup. Estimates of the prevalence of arthritis and other rheumatic conditions in the United States: Part I. *Arthritis Rheum* 2008;58(1):15–25.

*Opportunity may be disguised as misfortune*

*... when it is, stay alert:  Don't let yourself*

*overlook – or fail to recognize – the opportunity.*

-- Dr. Lena Cather

**Arthritis Pain ... *FREE!*:**
**Heal Arthritis Naturally – I Did, You Can, Too!**

SECTION II:  DEALING WITH ARTHRITIS

Chapter 1:  Management
Chapter 2:  Medical Consultation
Chapter 3:  Risk Factors
Chapter 4:  Physical Activity
Chapter 5:  Pain
Chapter 6:  Insomnia
Chapter 7:  Social Support

# SECTION II:  DEALING WITH ARTHRITIS
## Chapter 1:  Management

The focus of treatment for Arthritis is to control pain, minimize joint damage, and improve or maintain function and quality of life. According to the American College of Rheumatology, the treatment of Arthritis might involve the following:
   * Medication

   * Nonpharmacologic therapies
      * Physical or occupational therapy
      * Splints or joint assistive aids
      * Patient education and support
      * Weight loss

   * Surgery

In conjunction with medical treatment, self-management of Arthritis symptoms is very important as well.

The Arthritis Foundation Self-Help Program and the Chronic Disease Self-Management Program, both developed by Dr. Kate Lorig of Stanford University, are effective self-management education programs. These are just some of the programs that help people develop the skills needed to manage their Arthritis on a day-to-day basis and gain the confidence to carry it out.

*It's been my observation that, in most situations,*

*the solutions that are simplest*

*turn out to be the most effective.*

-- Dr. Lena Cather

# SECTION II: DEALING WITH ARTHRITIS
## Chapter 2: Medical Consultation

If you are diagnosed with Arthritis or other conditions, by all means consult a rheumatologist – an M.D. or a D.O. that specializes in the diagnosis and treatment of conditions and diseases involving joints, soft tissues, certain autoimmune diseases, and the allied conditions of connective tissues. Essentially, they medically treat diseases, disorders, etc., that affect the musculoskeletal system. This includes many autoimmune diseases, as these conditions often cause rheumatic issues.

Along with you medical management, you may want to consider talking with your rheumatologist about a referral to other helping professionals. These might include a chiropractor, an occupational therapist, home-care support, and a life coach or psychotherapist.

An occupational therapist can help with ideas to learn how to live your life better. Occupational therapy can be an important part of your medical care. It can help you learn to adjust to your life on a daily basis to take your Arthritis into account.

Before your appointment, be sure to check and see if occupational therapy when recommended by your doctor is covered by your health care insurance. Occupational therapists have a professional license and specialized training. So, it is possible – depending on your specifics of your insurance coverage – for occupational therapy to be a covered expense.

When you first start to deal with the arthritic pain, you may find that the most difficult thing that you are going to take on is not the pain. You may find that that what is most difficult is the loss of your independence. Arthritis can also lead to hand deformities that make many things difficult and may also confine you to a wheel chair later on.

Occupational therapists can either take care of you at your office or at your home. This will help you learn different techniques for personal grooming, dressing, getting in and out of bed, and even driving. With this help, you can maintain a level of independence necessary to conduct your life in an effective fashion.

There are other home-care help that can also be used to your advantage to avoid having to inhabit nursing homes or move in with relatives. Some communities have Meals on Wheels to help provide dinner. This is a service along with others that is going to help senior citizens who are looking to remain independent.

There are also services that send nurses to your home daily to help you with things and check your vital signs, give you medicine, and other help for you.

When you are dealing with Arthritis, some of these things may not be possible on your own without the help of services. Occupational help and other home care professionals can help you enjoy a happier, quality life.

A chiropractor can be helpful to keep your skeletal structure strong and in alignment. Since arthritis attacks joints, cartilage and the immune system, keeping your skeletal structure healthy and fully functioning helps the entire physical system function more effectively. Chiropractic or osteopathic manipulation is one of the recommendations sited later in this book.

It is also advisable for you to seek out Psychotherapy assistance. Life Coaching or Psychotherapy can enable you to better deal with the mental-emotional concomitants of chronic disease and chronic pain. Mental-emotional issues can include low self-esteem, pain management, grief recovery, relief of depression and despondency, and anger management. Getting help to better deal with these issues can beneficially affect the course of Arthritis on your body, as well.

As I mention in my solution-section of this book, I also highly recommend the use of a Hypnotherapist. Hypnosis is a valuable technique for reaching the subconscious mind, the deep part of the mind. Hypnosis can uncover deep-mind thought processes or ideas or blocks that might be underlying the Arthritic condition. Hypnosis can also help create pain relief, relaxation and an over-all generalized state of well-being.

Arthritis does not have to be the end of your happiness. Quite on the contrary! I encourage you to seek out adjunctive techniques and approaches to make absolutely certain that such is NOT the case! I urge you to make continued, ongoing happiness your steadfast goal – a goal upon which you refuse to compromise. I strongly support your 100% commitment to your happiness!

*You can never step into the same river;*

*For new waters are always flowing on to you.*

-- Heraclitus

# SECTION II:  DEALING WITH ARTHRITIS
## Chapter 3:  Risk Factors

Certain factors have been shown to be associated with a greater risk of Arthritis. Some of these risk factors are modifiable while others are not.

**Non-modifiable Risk Factors:**

*  **Age**: The risk of developing most types of Arthritis increases with age.

* **Gender**: Most types of Arthritis are more common in women; 60% of all people with Arthritis are women.  Gout is more common in men.

* **Genetic**: Specific genes are associated with a higher risk of certain types of Arthritis, such as Rheumatoid Arthritis (RA), Systemic Lupus Erythematous (SLE), and Ankylosing Spondylitis.

**Modifiable Risk Factors:**

* **Overweight and Obesity**: Excess weight can contribute to both the onset and progression of knee Osteoarthritis.

* **Joint Injuries**: Damage to a joint can contribute to the development of Osteoarthritis in that joint.

* **Infection**: Many microbial agents can infect joints and potentially cause the development of various forms of Arthritis.

* **Occupation**: Certain occupations involving repetitive knee bending and squatting are associated with Osteoarthritis of the knee.

# SECTION II: DEALING WITH ARTHRITIS
## Chapter 4: Physical Activity

**Physical activity: The Arthritis Pain Reliever**

Long gone are the days when health care providers told people with Arthritis to "rest their joints." In fact, physical activity can reduce pain and improve function, mobility, mood, and quality of life for most adults with many types of Arthritis including Osteoarthritis, Rheumatoid Arthritis, Fibromyalgia, and Lupus.

Physical activity can also help people with arthritis manage other chronic conditions such as diabetes, heart disease, and obesity. Most people with Arthritis can safely participate in a self-directed physical activity program or join one of many programs available in communities across the country. Some people may benefit from physical or occupational therapy.

**Benefits of Physical Activity for Adults with Arthritis**

Regular physical activity is just as important for people with arthritis or other rheumatic conditions as it is for all children and adults. Scientific studies have shown that participation in moderate-intensity, low-impact physical activity improves pain, function, mood, and quality of life without worsening symptoms or disease severity.

Being physically active can also delay the onset of disability if you have arthritis. But people with arthritis may have a difficult time being physically active because of symptoms (e.g., pain, stiffness), their lack of confidence in knowing how much and what to do, and unclear expectations of when they will see benefits. Both aerobic and muscle strengthening activities are proven to work well, and both are recommended for people with arthritis.

Public health agencies support physical activity as a self-management strategy for adults with Arthritis. On October 7, 2008, the Department of Health and Human Services released the new 2008 *Physical Activity Guidelines for Americans*. The Guidelines are based on the most up-to-date science regarding the health benefits of a physically active lifestyle.

These *Guidelines*, the first ever issued by the federal government, pertain to people of all ages and abilities including persons with chronic conditions such as Arthritis. On February 4, 2010, the Centers for Disease Control and Prevention and the

Arthritis Foundation released A National Public Health Agenda for Osteoarthritis that is a public health plan to address the most common type of Arthritis.

The Agenda lists physical activity as a priority intervention to improve Arthritis symptoms and prevent arthritis-related limitations in activity. In addition to public health agencies promoting physical activity to manage Arthritis, the American College of Rheumatology also recommends physical activity for almost all forms of Arthritis. The information that follows is based on these documents.

## Quantity of Physical Activity for Arthritis

### Why Is Physical Activity Important for Arthritis?
Scientific studies have shown that physical activity can reduce pain and improve function, mood, and quality of life for adults with arthritis. Physical activity can also help manage other chronic conditions that are common among adults with arthritis, such as diabetes, heart disease, and obesity.

### How Much Physical Activity Do Adults with Arthritis Need?
  * 2 hours and 30 minutes (150 minutes) of moderate-intensity aerobic activity per week OR
  * 1 hour 15 minutes (75 minutes) of vigorous-intensity aerobic activity per week OR
  * an equivalent combination* of moderate and vigorous activity.
AND
  * Muscle strengthening exercises on 2 or more days per week.
  * Balance exercises on 3 days per week if at risk of falling.

* A general rule is that 1 minute of vigorous intensity activity = 2 minutes of moderate intensity activity.

Aerobic activity is any activity that makes your heart beat faster and breathe a little harder than when you are sitting, standing, or lying.

Muscle strengthening activities should work all the major muscle groups (e.g., legs, hips, back, chest, abdomen, shoulders, and arms) of the body.

**Types of Physical Activity**
  * Low-impact aerobic activities including brisk walking, cycling, swimming, water aerobics, gardening, group exercise classes, dancing.

  * Muscle-strengthening exercises including calisthenics, weight training, and working with resistance bands. These can be done at home, in an exercise class, or at a fitness center.

  * Balance exercises including walking backwards, standing on one foot, and Tai Chi. If you are at risk of falling, balance exercises are included in many group exercise programs.


**Pain with Exercise**

Some soreness or aching in joints and surrounding muscles during and after exercise is normal for people with arthritis. This is especially true in the first 4 to 6 weeks of starting an exercise program. However, most people with arthritis find if they stick with exercise they will have significant long-term pain relief. Here are some tips to help you manage pain during and after exercise:
  * Modify your exercise program by reducing the frequency (days per week) or duration (amount of time each session) until pain improves.
  * Changing the type of exercise to reduce impact on the joints – for example switch from walking to water aerobics.
  * Do proper warm-up and cool-down before and after exercise.

* Exercise at a comfortable pace – you should be able to carry on a conversation while exercising.
* Make sure you have comfortable shoes that fit well.

Signs you should see your health care provider:
* Pain that is sharp, stabbing, and constant.
* Pain that causes you to limp.
* Pain that lasts more than 2 hours after exercise or gets worse at night.
* Pain that is not relieved by rest, medication, or hot/cold packs.
* Large increases in swelling or your joints feel "hot" or are red.

*Life is really simple, but*

*we insist on making it complicated*

-- Confucius

# SECTION II: DEALING WITH ARTHRITIS
## Chapter 5: Pain

Having pain is your body's way of telling you that something is wrong. For some people, they say "no pain, no gain"; hence, for them, pain is a sign that they have done something to the point of destruction. The body will let you know this.

If you are suffering from arthritis you have pain in the joints. This can keep you from doing the things that you want to. It is important to have pain management so that you can deal with the arthritis and live from day to day with hardly any frustration.

Like a red flashing light, your pain in the body is going to signal that you need to stop what you are doing and take action about your body's health. Pain is very natural and it does not have to be hard for you. There are a number of things that can cause arthritic pain.

Pain can be caused by inflammation in the joints. This type of pain is usually joined by redness and swelling in younger patients or anyone that just develops a condition. A second cause is damage to the joint tissue. A person usually feels as though s/he has pulled a muscle when this type of pain is occurring. It can be a condition due to stress on a joint or it can be caused by other problems.

Pain can also happen from fatigue. You may simply have a small amount of lingering pain; being tired can make you have this more.  Think of it in terms of a headache at the end of the day when you are tired.  Joint pain works in the same way.

Depression and stress can cause pain or make your pain more severe than it really is.  This is a terrible cycle to start.  You will get depressed when you have pain and this will cause you to be more depressed which will cause you to feel even worse.

Arthritic pain in people is likely to fell a lot different than other kinds of pain.  It is important to have a pain management system.  This will also include eating healthy and exercising better to improve the condition.  Taking medication will also help.  You may also want to use massage to help you with your arthritis as well.

Staying optimistic about your outlook for life and taking on the challenge of pain when it comes can vastly increase your mental-emotional health and well-being.  Arthritis, certainly, can be very hard.  At the same time, keeping a positive mindset will take you a long way toward overcoming it and creating a normal life for yourself.

# SECTION II: DEALING WITH ARTHRITIS
## Chapter 6: Insomnia

If you are dealing with arthritis, one of the hardest things to deal with is the insomnia. The sleeping disorder is going to prevent you from getting the rest that you need to stay healthy and this will in return make your arthritis worse.

This can be a terrible cycle with which to deal. There are many things that you can do to affect your arthritic condition. It is vitally important to consider all of the options so that you can get a better night's rest every time you go to bed.

Having insomnia can be caused by a number of problems. You might have difficulty falling asleep. Many people will experience this at some point in their life. However, if you are frequently finding it hard to drift off to sleep, you may want to talk to your doctor about it.

If you are waking up often – and for no good reason – throughout the night, this might be a symptom too. It may indicate a deeper, more underlying cause. For example, this can happen to everyone from time to time. It can be a common experience for new parents. If you find yourself tossing and turning more than once a week, you are probably dealing with insomnia.

Some with insomnia will sleep throughout the night. Their problem may be that they wake up too early or they do not feel refreshed after many hours of sleep. Depending on how frequently insomnia happens for you, you might be diagnosed with short-term insomnia, intermittent insomnia or chronic insomnia.

Anyone that suffers from arthritis will also find that they have chronic insomnia or insomnia that does not go away, occurring for a long time period. There are many reasons that chronic insomnia is found in people with arthritis.

The pain keeps some arthritis sufferers awake at night. In addition, some arthritics find that their joints are painful and inflamed after doing activity.

A second reason for insomnia in those with arthritis is a high level of stress that most patients with arthritis have. Worrying about an appointment with a doctor can cause a person to stay awake all night long.

Insomnia can equally affect a patient who is young or one who is old. Insomnia can also equally affect an arthritic who has been recently diagnosed as it can someone who has had the problem of arthritis for many years.

Insomnia can be a side effect of the medicine that is being used to treat the illness. While some medicines can be helpful in reducing pain, they can also result in all-night-long insomnia. Of course, without taking medication, sleep might still be impossible. Pain, by itself, can prevent good, solid sleep.

There are a number of steps to take to eliminate insomnia. The first step is to recognize that you are NOT alone. Talk to your doctor about any medications that you might be taking that keep you up all night. Look for alternatives. Discuss these with your doctor, as well. Experiment to find what might work for you.

One effective procedure is to create a sleep-time ritual. This is especially beneficial if you have trouble falling asleep. Set a specific time for your sleep-time ritual to begin – in this way your mind and body begin to recognize this time as a signal to begin to unwind and relax. Relaxation is one of the necessary precursors to falling asleep.

Then, once you have selected your time, begin your sleep-time ritual. First, you would want to turn off any cares or burdens of the day. Then, your ritual might include taking a long, luxurious, relaxing bath; or you might drink some Sleepy-time tea or warm milk. You might sit in a rocking chair for 15 minutes and rock to your favorite soft music. You might read for 15 minutes from your favorite inspirational book. You get the idea – you take this time to engage in activities that are specifically relaxing to you.

Then, you get into bed … allow your body to snuggle into the softness of the mattress. Adjust your position to maximum comfort … and put your mind on one relaxing activity. For example, you might imagine yourself on the beach, watching as each wave comes in and breaks on the sand … and continue to do so until you fall asleep.

Taking the right steps to take the stress out of your life is going to help you sleep better at night, too. Pay attention to the events that cause you stress … just notice what they are.

Then, systematically, eliminate the ones that you can. If you cannot put your mind at ease about the ones that remain, consult a qualified psychotherapist to assist you in this regard.

You and your doctor are the only people that can take the right course of action to fix the insomnia in your life. Talk to your doctor about it and create a solid plan that WORKS! Getting a good night's sleep is an essential part of healthy living.

# SECTION II:  DEALING WITH ARTHRITIS
## Chapter 7:  Social Support

There are millions of Americans that suffer from the pain of arthritis and related conditions all the time.  Many patients who suffer from arthritis feel as though they are alone and confused.  It is important to know that you are not alone in this suffering.

Arthritis can be a very difficult disease to understand.  This adds to feeling confused about what is happening to you and about what to do about it.  When you feel like you are the only one going through this disease, it can help to remind yourself that there are many others that feel the same way that you do.

You might choose to meet and talk to others that are dealing with the same painful arthritis conditions.  Joining one of the many different arthritis support groups might help you feel better about your condition and help your outlook on life.

One vital aspect to keep in mind for you on your quest: Surround yourself with positive people.  The more you immerse yourself in positive energy – and stay away from nay-sayers and negativity – the easier it becomes for you to reap the powerful healing benefits that these positive energies bring.

The Arthritis Foundation is one of the non-profit organizations that were formed for those that have arthritis. There are over 100 different conditions that are related to arthritis and this foundation has worked hard to meet those needs and concerns for people.

This organization can provide you with information about arthritic conditions. It can also work as an advocate for the patients that are dealing with arthritis. It sponsors medical research for the condition and joins with other organizations and companies to bring patients the services that they need. To learn more, just visit **http://arthritis.org**

When you are looking for something on a personal level, you can find a local arthritis group. Ask your doctor or call your local hospital. Often hospitals sponsor these types of support groups. A local group can allow you to meet with others that are dealing with arthritis. It can provide you with ideas on how to cope in daily life.

You can also check you local newspapers or look online for ideas on where to find such community support groups. You can even start your own group! If no support group exists in your town, there may be a huge need for someone to head up this type of project.

A support group is also an important resource for children who are suffering from arthritis. Since arthritis is a condition that is often associated with age, a child with arthritis might be even more prone to feelings of isolation. Belonging to a children's support group can provide an antidote for such feelings. The children's wing of your local hospital may be able to help you find such a support group for your child.

Age is no deterrent for the disease of arthritis. All age groups can benefit from social support for effective treatment and healing!

Flow with whatever may happen and let your mind be free.

Stay centered by accepting whatever you are doing.

This is the ultimate.

-- Zhuangzi (Chinese philosopher)

**Arthritis Pain ... *FREE!*:**
**Heal Arthritis Naturally – I Did, You Can, Too!**

# PART III: MY PERSONAL JOURNEY
# SECTION I: RECENT SCIENTIFIC DISCOVERIES

In the 30 years since I've enjoyed being healed from Rheumatoid Arthritis, science has undertaken massive research, uncovered numerous discoveries, and formulated even-more numerous theories based on this research and the ensuing discoveries. This represents a vast amount of data and theoretical explanations.

The Good News for me – and for this book – is that the results of these most-recent scientific explorations have given me an explanation of why I experienced the healing outcomes that I did! I totally believe in the existence – and experience – of miracles. However, while the explanation of miraculous was totally acceptable to me – namely, that my healing from Rheumatoid Arthritis was a miracle – I fully recognize that there are those among you who might appreciate a fuller, more-detailed, less-nebulous explanation of the facts.

Science has caught up with (my) experience, and I feel that I can now provide just such a clear, detailed explanation. If you are not inclined to find science absolutely and utterly intriguing and fascinating, you can choose to skip this section … and resume reading at the next Section – "Section II: Specific Steps to Healing". In that Section, I reveal the exact steps that worked for me to heal the Rheumatoid Arthritis from which I had suffered for so many years.

## Scientific Revelations: Existence in Ten Dimensions

Recent research findings in Science reveal that reality exists in ten (10) or more dimensions. There is length … and width … and height … and duration/time … and 6 more dimensions that have not been fully described as yet.

This theorizing expands the old idea of 3 dimensions – length and width and height. It is a significant advancement, even, on the more-recent idea of 4 dimensions – length and width and height and time/duration.

Since scientific discoveries have now identified the existence of 10 dimensions, it is totally feasible that there could be many, many more dimensions … as yet undiscovered. This leads the way to speculation of a view of our universe in which there are unlimited possibilities … as yet unexplored and undiscovered!

To extend this a little further, it is totally feasible to me that one of these as-yet-undiscovered dimensions could be the dimension of healing. Since our universe is one of unlimited possibilities, it opens the door to healing as a serious and distinct possibility!

The discovery of our universe having 10 dimensions is such a revolutionary concept that we cannot even mentally comprehend HOW all of these dimensions can exist and what exactly their existence means in terms of our day-to-day life! Actually, scientists themselves do not yet agree on how to even represent such a 10-dimensional universal view!  Certain scientists have arrived at models that suggest such a representation – each model being different, of course; but, even as these models attempt to clarify the concepts, they expand the mind beyond what we can totally grasp.

It is totally revolutionary and incredibly amazing!  However, it does point out that there are realities in existence in our Universe that are beyond our understanding … and they are even beyond the comprehension of trained scientific minds.

So, enter the concept that we cannot totally explain – in scientific terms – all of the outcomes that exist in everyday life!

## Scientific Revelations:  Einstein's Theory of Relativity

Current findings in Science – among them, superstring theory, a modern attempt to explain all of the particles and fundamental forces of nature in one theory – far surpass Albert Einstein's Theory of Relativity.  And this, despite the fact that Einstein's Theory was utterly revolutionary when it was introduced and advanced by its proponents!

In a startling departure from previously accepted theory in physics and mechanics, in 1905, Albert Einstein proposed mass-energy equivalence.  In his Theory of Relativity, Einstein described the following relationship:  $E = mc^2$ (e = energy, m = mass at rest, c = the constant of the speed of light in a vacuum, a suitable conversion factor to transform units of mass to units of energy).

This equation describes Einstein's concept that the mass of a body is a measure of its energy content -- energy and mass are equivalent and transmutable. In other words, Einstein had discovered that everything in our physical universe that has mass -- everything that appears dense and solid and visible -- is energy. All that we experience as solid matter is really a combination of energy forces combining small subatomic particles – neutrons, protons, and electrons. Breaking this down even more, the cosmos, the universe, the earth, humans, organ systems, cells, molecules, atoms, subatomic particles -- all, are energy.

According to Einstein's conception, energy existed as particles which when observed "appeared to be" a solid mass although it was only due to the high rate of vibration that subatomic particles create giving them the "appearance" of solidity. All things when seen in their basic form consist of energy ... and a HUGE amount of energy, at that! The constant of the speed of light is an extremely LARGE number. Squaring it – multiplying it by itself -- makes this quantity one that is HUGE!

From the 1920s on, science investigated nuclear realities. It supported the fact that all matter is comprised of vast energy-components. In other words, all that we experience as solid matter is really a combination of energy forces combining small particles – neutrons, protons and electrons.

Einstein's Theory of Relativity stated that energy is not destroyed, that it merely changes form. Since all that has matter exists as energy – or, has vast energy components – and energy has the capability to change forms, it opens the door to the understanding that one of those forms of energy is the energy-form of thought.

# Scientific Revelations: Mind-Body Connection

## Mind-Body Medicine

The term "mind-body medicine" has recently become used to depict the connections between psychological, behavioral, and sociocultural processes with all levels of biological functioning -- from the organ systems, to the cellular, to the molecular -- and with health. A central tenet of mind–body medicine is the recognition that the mind plays a key role in health and that any presumed separation of mind and body is false.

## Research Literature in Mind-Body Medicine

The literature on mind–body medicine comprises more than 2000 peer-reviewed studies published in the past 25 years. The groundwork for understanding the physiology of mind–body interactions was established by pioneering studies in the 1930s by Walter Cannon. Cannon (Cannon, W.B. The Wisdom of the Body. New York: W.W.Norton, 1932: 218-242) documented the physiological effects of what he termed the "emergency reaction," which he defined as an acute physiologic reaction that prepares the organism for fighting or fleeing. Cannon described the physiologic changes associated with the fight or-flight response as being characterized by increased sympathetic nervous system activity, increased central nervous system arousal, and increased skeletal-muscle activity.

## Additional Research in Mind-Body Connection

A huge discovery was made in 1974.

In that year, documented evidence of a physiological link between the mind and body was firmly established. Robert Ader, Ph.D., an experimental psychologist at the University of Rochester Medical Center, made a surprise discovery while investigating conditioned response in rats (a variation of Pavlov's classic research). Dr. Ader found that the rats had been conditioned not only to associate sweet water with nausea (his experimental hypothesis), but also with an immune shutdown.

To Dr. Ader and to those scientists who have followed up on his research, the conclusion was obvious: The minds of the animals were controlling their immune systems. This finding led to the development of the new, hybrid field of psychoneuroimmunology (PNI).

However, even after this crucial discovery, the central question of just how the mind and body were connected still remained unclear. Resolution of this question occurred in 1981 also at the University of Rochester with the work of David Felten, M.D., Ph.D., and his team of researchers.

Using special fluorescent stains to trace nerves to various bodily locations, including bone marrow, lymph nodes, and the spleen, Dr. Felten and his team discovered a network of nerves leading to blood vessels as well as cells of the immune system. They looked at a tissue sample from the spleen and there saw a network of nerve fibers from the central nervous system (the wiring that leads to the brain), together with white blood cells (key players in the immune system).

The researchers also found nerves in the thymus and spleen terminating near clusters of lymphocytes, macrophages, and mast cells. All of these cells help control immune function.

Dr. Felten and his team of researchers had discovered a hard-wire connection between the body's immune system and the central nervous system under control of the brain. This finding provided additional hard data to prove the mind-body connection. There it was: the mind-body connection – clear evidence that the brain has the ability to send signals to immune-system cells.


**Scientific Revelations: Brain Science Research**

Let's get back to considering the energy aspects of thought and thinking. The idea that thought is an energy form is supported by new findings in the realm of Brain Research, which has seen a recent explosion of research aimed at explaining the intricate workings of the human brain.

With the advent of brand new advanced-imaging equipment, Neuroscientists are now able to literally "see" how the brain responds to stimuli. They can see this stimuli-drive brain response in the very act of that response occurring!

A few of the most-recent brain-science discoveries include the fact that thoughts are things ... and that these thoughts lead to feelings and behaviors. Thinking and thoughts are biological, electrochemical impulses; as such, they are forms of energy. Through the use of functional MRI (fMRI), they can now be seen, measured, and examined. Thoughts are real.

By understanding brain function, the mind can be controlled; thinking can be controlled. Once thinking is controlled, behavior can, complementarily, be controlled.

### Scientific Revelations: Neurogenesis/Brain Plasticity

One of the greatest neuroscience discoveries of all time was made in 1997. This discovery is known as Neurogenesis, or Brain Plasticity. Neurogenesis refers to the fact that not only is the brain capable of producing new connections between its nerve cells, but it also has the ability to generate entirely new neurons. In other words, the brain is not hardwired – it is imminently flexible! The brain can be changed!

If the brain is stimulated – e.g., by learning new things – it physically forms and grows new neural connections. These new connections will increase the total number of neural connections within the brain and, as a result, increase the brain's capacity for achievement.

This fantastic news opens the door to destroying any neuron patterns that have been firing thoughts saying, "I can't". All those excuses need to go! And, in their place, it is suggested that beneficial outcomes can ensue from replacing them with neuron patterns that fire thoughts saying, "I can"! It's a scientific truth: there is no limit on your capacity to achieve new things.

In addition, in 2007, researchers seeking help for Alzheimer's determined that intentionally stimulating the brain to do new things and create new connections caused the brain to build up a "neural reserve". It is theorized that this reserve could be called upon to replace brain cells damaged by either pathological or atrophic Alzheimer's. The actualization of this still remains to be seen.

## SUMMARY:

As far as my Healing Journey is concerned, the following scientific findings apply directly to the outcomes of healing! Here's how ...

**The Universe in which we live is unlimited**
- -- the scientific discovery that reality exists in 10-or-more Dimensions and, as such, that there are incredible, unexplored possibilities in the Universe
  - -- as a corollary, this points out that there are scientific results known conceptually that still cannot yet be accurately explained.

**Matter exists as Energy**
- -- Einstein's theory of Relativity states that all matter exists as energy

**Thoughts are Energy forms**
- -- Brain-Science explains that thoughts are biological, electrochemical impulses; these can now be seen, measured, examined and used to explain thought
  - -- the finding that thoughts as forms of energy are real; thoughts are things

**Thoughts & their resultant behaviors can be controlled**
   -- Brain-Science has found that thoughts lead to feelings
      and behaviors
      -- by understanding brain function, thinking and the mind
         can be controlled
      -- once thinking is controlled, behavioral outcomes can be
         controlled
**Existence of the Brain-Mind-Body connection**
   -- discovery of the brain-mind-body connection:  how
      thoughts create direct effects in the body
**The brain is not fixed, it is flexible**
   -- the brain is not hardwired – it is imminently flexible
   -- the brain produces new connections and can generate
      entirely new nerve cells
      -- new learning forms new neural connections
      -- new connections increase the total number of neural
                              connections
      -- new connections increase brain's capacity for
         achievement
      -- unused connections weaken and, ultimately,
         deteriorate, becoming totally unusable

So, the Universe is awash with unlimited possibilities and is
comprised of energy.  Other energy forms can affect the
Universe.  Most notably for our purposes, it can be affected
by the energy-form of thought.  Thought has been shown to
affect what happens in the body.  Learning creates new
brain-nervous system connections and enhances the brain's
capacity to achieve new outcomes ... these outcomes can,
in turn, be reflected in the state of health of the body.

In the realm of Brain Science, It's a scientific truth: there is
no limit on your capacity to achieve new things!

# PART III: MY PERSONAL JOURNEY
# SECTION II: SPECIFIC STEPS TO HEALING

The specific steps that comprise my Healing from Rheumatoid Arthritis were a combination of creating balance in all of the aspects of my being:

A.  Mental:  Productive Use of the Mind

B.  Spiritual:  the Life-giving Energy the brings the Mind, the Emotions and the Body together as an Interactive Whole Being

C.  Emotional:  Harmony in the Emotions

D.  Physical:  Healthy Body Functioning

I say a "combination" because there was no ONE thing … it was a blend of multiple steps.  As I reflect back on my experience, I am not aware of one aspect being more important than another.  I believe that it was interplay between all four of these aspects that resulted in the gestalt – or total – healing that I enjoy to this day.

Let me also say that where the Mind, the Emotions, the Spirit, and the Body are concerned, I do not experience that there are clear-cut differentiations.  I like to tell my clients – and I have witnessed this repeatedly as true – that the Mind and Body interact seamlessly.  In other words, I do not know where the Body begins and the Mind stops, or where the Mind begins and the Body stops.  In my experience, they operate in tandem.

Now I would like to extend this idea: I do not know how to differentiate between what is Mental and what is Emotional and what is Spiritual and what is Physical. I seems to me – from repeated observation and personal research – that what we each have operating is a Mental-Emotional-Spiritual-Physical complex!

So, with that said, I will still break these areas down for you. I do so, to provide organization and to make it more possible for me to talk about each area, not because I really experience these as discrete areas:

## MY HEALING STEPS:  TIME-LINE

A.  MENTAL:
    Step #1 -- Mind:  Conscious and Subconscious (1968-71)
    Step #2 – Affirmations           (1973)
    Step #3 -- Attitude:  Outlook of Perfect Health   (1974)

B.  SPIRITUAL:
    Step #4 – Meditation         (1968 & earlier)
    Step #5 – Prayer         (1968 & earlier)
    Step #6 – Forgiveness         (1969)
    Step #7 -- Universal Laws         (1975)

C.  MENTAL-PHYSICAL:
    Step #8 – Exercise         (1968 & earlier)

D.  MENTAL-EMOTIONAL:
    Step #9 --Thoughts => Feelings         (1976)
    Step #10 -- Acceptance and Self-care         1977)
    Step #11 --Hypnotherapeutic Clearing:
        Uncover faulty belief => Release        1978)

E.  MENTAL-PHYSICAL (cont'd):
    Step #12 – Breathing        (1960-1977)
    Step #13 – Relaxation        (1978)

F.  PHYSICAL:
    Step #14 -- Hair Analysis => vitamin & mineral
                supplementation        (1979)
    Step #15 -- Edgar Cayce Remedies        (1980)
    Step #16 -- Healthy Food Selection:  Diet        (1980)

The first 10 Steps describe practices that I developed into the basic foundation for living my life. I continue these Steps – along with modifications and refinements of them – to this day. These basic foundation Steps were important to "set the stage" for the ultimate Healing that I experienced.

Steps #11 through #16 are specific treatment approaches that helped me to rid my life of Rheumatoid Arthritis. I would like to point out once again that none of these Steps were enacted in a vacuum. It is my firm belief that the healing that I experienced came about through the combined action of each of these Steps ... together with all of the other Steps.

# PART III: MY PERSONAL JOURNEY
## SECTION III: TAKING THE STEPS

### Introduction

As I mentioned in Part I of this book, during my 14 years (1966 - 1980) of dealing with the effects of chronic pain and arthritic disease, I completed a Bachelor of Science degree and a Master of Science degree. Both of these were in the fields of Psychology and Human Behavior.

So, along with my own personal Arthritis-related challenges, I was in the position to learn new things, to research new ideas, and to make new discoveries for myself and for others in the realm of the human psyche – the mind-body-emotion-spirit complex. This part of my journey was great! It was intriguing. It was mystical! It was exciting!

I love learning! For me, the most fascinating areas of learning include learning about the incredible workings of the human mind and of the human being!

I've often commented – somewhat in jest – that, as a very young child, I wore my mother to a frazzle by incessantly asking her, "Why do I have to do it that way?" and "Why is it like this?" and "Why did s/he say that?" and "Why does this happen?" and "Why, Mommy???"

You get the picture!

Well, in the field of psychology, I found the PERFECT outlet for getting my delightful curiosity satisfied. Since I am working to help people make their lives better, I have carte-blanche permission to ask, "Why?" to my heart's content (any of my clients reading this would readily tell you that this is precisely what I do!). Better yet – people are happy to tell me!

So, while I was battling the daily effects of my own chronic illness and unrelenting pain, I was in the position to learn about – and investigate – healing and the components that are requisite for optimal health. Of course, since the mind, emotions, body and spirit interact so intensely, these ideas about healing include emotional methods, mental ideas, physical practices and spiritual techniques.

This pathway was not a straightforward, move ahead course. I had many days that were one step forward, two steps back. And I had many days that were two steps forward, one step back! There were also some two-step-forward days!!

I recall one of those former days, when it was one step forward and two steps back …

I had been in University classes all day and it was late afternoon. As I was driving back to my apartment near the University, I felt totally exhausted. It was not just a feeling of incredible fatigue, I felt as though I had absolutely no energy.

It was as though every ounce of physical energy had drained out and deserted me. My body felt as though it had shut off … and it was being followed closely by my mind. As I approached a red light, I had a flash thought, "I don't think I have the energy to move my foot onto the brake."

It did not feel as though I was commenting about a possibility ... it felt like a certainty. In the fleeting second that remained, I found myself having a dialog with myself, "If you don't stop, you will cause damage ... you will hit that car in front of you." and "I will just have to hit it ... I have no energy to get my foot over onto the brake." and "You can't do that!"

I am happy to report that I had trained my subconscious mind QUITE effectively to drive the car. When I got to that decision-making last second, with no intervening thought whatsoever, my foot lifted onto the brake and pressed down. Yes, happily enough ... ! However, this left me shaken ... and shaking.

This experience left me more dynamically and painfully aware of additional – dangerous – aspects of my condition ...

Below, I explain my Journey to Healing. You will notice that I do so in some detail. I include all the information you need to be able to duplicate for yourself the Success I've experienced. I do so that you can understand all the Steps that worked for me.

I want you to be able – if you so choose – to undertake this Healing Journey yourself. In addition, I want you to make the full Journey in a MUCH abbreviated period of time. By telling you what worked – and what didn't work – It's my intention to shorten your Journey. I'm taking the "guess work" out of it for you!

What follows in Chapter 1 through Chapter 5 is the learning-and-growth Healing Path that I took for the first 13 of those 14 years; Chapter 6 describes the culmination in year 14.

*I want you to be everything that is you,*

*deep at the center of your being.*

-- Confucius

# PART III:  MY PERSONAL JOURNEY
## SECTION III:  TAKING THE STEPS

### Chapter I:  Specific Steps to Healing – Mental

**Step #1 -- Mind:  Conscious and Subconscious**
**(1968 – 1971:  BS degree studies)**

The human mind has two parts -- your conscious mind and your subconscious mind.  Each has very specific roles that it performs for you.

Your conscious mind is the part of your mind that you are aware with most of the time.  It is logical, judgmental, analytical and critical.  Usually, it is your conscious mind that gets over-involved in wanting to control everything.  For most people, this comes from a lack of a specific type of confidence -- namely, confidence in things working out well, in the orderliness of the Universe, in their own VERY CREATIVE abilities to cope with what occurs ... and make a successful conclusion.

Your subconscious mind is very different from your conscious mind.  Your subconscious mind has memory of events that have occurred in your life.  In addition, it operates as a very-obedient servant -- in other words, it creates that which it is commanded to create.

So, how do you usually give commands to your subconscious mind?  You do this through your thoughts.  What you think becomes a command to your subconscious mind. Remember that it is your servant? It does not argue with you. It simply proceeds to create that which you have told it about a situation.

This principle is the basis of "self-fulfilling prophecy". You create that which you have told yourself in a given situation.

Let's look at what this means: If you have told yourself (and your subconscious mind, which is just sitting there, listening in) something POSITIVE, this can lead to a VERY GOOD, self-confident, self-esteeming event. Your subconscious mind can proceed to create a positive outcome in your life! Your subconscious mind can help you begin to build your sense of positive self-esteem.

On the other hand, if you have told yourself some NEGATIVE thought -- something you don't even WANT to experience ... guess what? You are correct: Your subconscious mind then proceeds to activate the negative thought, too.

And WHY is this? It occurs specifically because your subconscious mind is trying to do what it was told! It is trying to please you -- and it thinks it can do so by following your commands, which you delivered via your thoughts!
What a pickle, right? It sure is ... because, not only are you focusing on what you DON'T want – and increasing the probability that it will occur, but also it FEELS BAD. And YOU feel bad as a result!

So, what else could you do?

# PART III: MY PERSONAL JOURNEY
# SECTION III: TAKING THE STEPS

## Introduction

As I mentioned in Part I of this book, during my 14 years (1966 - 1980) of dealing with the effects of chronic pain and arthritic disease, I completed a Bachelor of Science degree and a Master of Science degree. Both of these were in the fields of Psychology and Human Behavior.

So, along with my own personal Arthritis-related challenges, I was in the position to learn new things, to research new ideas, and to make new discoveries for myself and for others in the realm of the human psyche – the mind-body-emotion-spirit complex. This part of my journey was great! It was intriguing. It was mystical! It was exciting!

I love learning! For me, the most fascinating areas of learning include learning about the incredible workings of the human mind and of the human being!

I've often commented – somewhat in jest – that, as a very young child, I wore my mother to a frazzle by incessantly asking her, "Why do I have to do it that way?" and "Why is it like this?" and "Why did s/he say that?" and "Why does this happen?" and "Why, Mommy???"

You get the picture!

Well, in the field of psychology, I found the PERFECT outlet for getting my delightful curiosity satisfied. Since I am working to help people make their lives better, I have carte-blanche permission to ask, "Why?" to my heart's content (any of my clients reading this would readily tell you that this is precisely what I do!). Better yet – people are happy to tell me!

So, while I was battling the daily effects of my own chronic illness and unrelenting pain, I was in the position to learn about – and investigate – healing and the components that are requisite for optimal health. Of course, since the mind, emotions, body and spirit interact so intensely, these ideas about healing include emotional methods, mental ideas, physical practices and spiritual techniques.

This pathway was not a straightforward, move ahead course. I had many days that were one step forward, two steps back. And I had many days that were two steps forward, one step back! There were also some two-step-forward days!!

I recall one of those former days, when it was one step forward and two steps back …

I had been in University classes all day and it was late afternoon. As I was driving back to my apartment near the University, I felt totally exhausted. It was not just a feeling of incredible fatigue, I felt as though I had absolutely no energy.

It was as though every ounce of physical energy had drained out and deserted me. My body felt as though it had shut off … and it was being followed closely by my mind. As I approached a red light, I had a flash thought, "I don't think I have the energy to move my foot onto the brake."

You could do what I did. I became VERY vigilant of my thoughts. I started to pay very close attention to whatever I was thinking. I did this with the knowledge that, left unchanged, those thoughts would be created by my subconscious mind.

I especially watched for thoughts about my health. I purposely began thinking thoughts of being healthy and totally well. Even though this was not yet the case, I recognized that – to get me there – I had to get my subconscious mind started on that track!

I felt much, much better – repeating to myself thoughts of strong, complete health … than I ever had when I thought about the disabling pain of arthritis. The truth of the matter is that I felt more hopeful when I focused on myself enjoying strong, complete health. I felt more self-confidence; I felt as though I had new possibilities.

At the same time, for all the time that I had repeated negative possibilities to myself, I recognized that I was able to see and appreciate HOW INCREDIBLY WELL my subconscious mind had been bringing things into being ... just the way I'd negatively predicted they would be! How eye opening this was for me!

If I could influence so effectively the outcomes in the direction of negative, ill-health, it struck me as totally conceivable that I could be equally effective in creating healthy results, too! Once I started appreciating the amazing creative power of my subconscious mind, it became a much easier task to start directing that creation positively ... in ways that would serve my goals!

## Step #2 – Affirmations  (1973)

Affirmations take the principle of the creative power of the subconscious mind and formulate it into ACTION. Affirmations are constructed of positive phrases.

Not just any positive phrases, however!

Affirmations use the positive phrases that are specific to the outcomes that I desired in my life.  So, to construct affirmations, I carefully decided the results that I most wanted to experience.  Since what I wanted was to be pain-free, I constructed affirmative statements that described JUST THAT!

Some of the healing affirmations that produced markedly beneficial outcomes for me included:
1. I embrace the feeling of total comfort in my body & mind!
2. I know that my body is able to totally heal of itself!
3. I do what it takes to support my body to attain state of complete healing!
4. I joyfully release all blocks and barriers to my total good health!
5. I willingly accept complete healing in my being now!

## Step #3 -- Attitude:  Outlook of Perfect Health (1974)

Attitude is a way of looking at an event, or a series of events -- a specific way of thinking, a specific mind-set.  An attitude is an evaluation of a particular event or occurrence. Attitudes may be regarded as predispositions, and are at their best when directly connected to behavior.

Affect, cognition, and action are the three aspects of attitude. The affective response is an emotional response that expresses the degree of preference for an entity. The behavioral intention is a verbal indication or typical behavioral tendency of an individual. The cognitive response is a cognitive evaluation of the entity that constitutes your beliefs about the object.

My attitude for the healing that I experienced was a strong, solid outlook of complete and total health for my body, my mind, my emotions and my spirit. I was enthusiastic about this! I eagerly embraced complete health on all levels of my being – physically, mentally, emotionally and spiritually.

*So it is with minds. Unless you keep them busy
with some definite subject that will bridle and
control them, they throw themselves in disorder ...
in the vague field of imagination ... and there is
no fancy that they do not bring forth in the agitation.*

-- Michel de Montaigne

# PART III:   MY PERSONAL JOURNEY
## SECTION III:  TAKING THE STEPS

### Chapter 2:  Specific Steps to Healing – Spiritual

**Step #4 – Meditation  (1968 & earlier)**

I was introduced to Meditation early in my spiritual development.  I first started meditating while I was still a teenager.  I was very fortunate to have experienced a strong religious affiliation from the time I was a child; this gave me the opportunity to grow up with it – contributing both positive values and strong moral beliefs … all of these I readily embraced.  It also gave me practice both in ritual and in an intense, experiential knowledge of my own Inner Life.

So, when I was introduced to the idea of formalized Meditation, I took to it easily.  It felt totally natural to me.  It allowed – and continues to allow -- me a time of stillness and tranquility, a time for reflection and the experience of energy realities, a time of balance and harmony.  I love it!

Getting into a state of Meditation became a skill in which I delighted.  Being in the meditative state allowed me a healing place for my emotions, my mind, and my energy being.  Meditation allowed my body to tap into its own wisdom, where the necessary steps to healing were encoded.

Meditation is a family of practices in which the practitioner trains his or her mind to self-induce a mode of consciousness in order to realize some benefit.  This state of consciousness is relaxed, still, and intense.

Usually, Meditation is an internal, personal practice, done without any external involvement, except perhaps prayer beads to count prayers. There are dozens-or-more different styles of meditation practice. Meditation has been practiced since antiquity as a component of numerous religious traditions, especially in monastic settings.

Since the 1960s, meditation has been the focus of increasing scientific research, of uneven rigor and quality. In over 1,000 published research studies, various methods of meditation have been linked to changes in metabolism, blood pressure, brain activation, and other bodily processes. Meditation has been used in clinical settings as a method of stress and pain reduction.

So, just when I needed a vehicle for healing, regular Meditation practice became a keystone to "fill the bill". Meditation gave me focus, and renewed – re-energized – my body and mind. All of which, in my experience, are important components of healing.


**Step #5 – Prayer  (1968 & earlier)**

Prayer is a form of religious practice that, through deliberate practice, seeks to activate a rapport to spiritual aspects. Prayer may be either individual or communal; it can take place in public or in private.

The beliefs about prayer to which I adhere are the following:
  * prayer is intended to impart certain attitudes in the one
     who prays

* prayer aims to affect the very fabric of reality as I (the pray-er) perceive it
* prayer is a catalyst for change in oneself and/or one's circumstances, or those of third-party beneficiaries
* prayer is a statement of positive intent
* prayer is a vehicle for creativity

For me, prayer is another form of alteration of consciousness, which allows my mind-emotions-body complex to enter a state of harmony with my spiritual being. Hence, prayer can create the ideal state of mind that is strongly conducive to healing – physical, mental, emotional and spiritual.

There are many different types of prayer. My preferred use for prayer is for gratitude and appreciation. In a basic tenet propounded by the psychological theory of Behaviorism, what is reinforced is strengthened. This concept serves as another application of the creative activity of the subconscious mind – namely, to create that which our thoughts direct it to create. So, if we focus with gratitude, we establish the very attitude that creates more for which to be grateful!

## Step #6 – Forgiveness (1969)

Forgiveness is the act of releasing the pressure and burden from past hurts. It is a mental-emotional energy-action that can fashion profoundly-powerful results on the spiritual and physical levels. Stated another way, forgiveness has the power to heal.

Now, when I examined my own use of forgiveness, I did not find huge areas of my life where I was carrying – gunny-sacking – resentments from the past. Rather, I used forgiveness as an on-going method to PREVENT there being any residue from the past.

The one area of forgiveness that was important to my ultimate healing was to forgive MYSELF for false beliefs and for misunderstandings that I had mistakenly held onto from the past. So, once I had learned – and used – hypnotherapy to create effective release from false understandings about the past, I applied forgiveness to myself for having believed these misunderstandings for so long. I did this so as to not create resentment toward myself.


**Step #7 -- Universal Laws:  Law of Attraction (1975)**

The creative action of the subconscious mind – namely, to create that about which a person thinks – can be viewed as the description of creativity in operation on the microcosmic level. It is the way I – and each of us – create outcomes in my – our – personal sphere.

For the operation of the Universe-as-a-whole, there is a higher-level of creative operation. The Principle of Universal Creativity describes the operation of creativity on a Macrocosmic level. This Universal Principle can be termed the Law of Attraction.

The Law of Attraction states that positive and negative thinking bring about positive and negative physical results, respectively. It is the Law of Cause and Effect in action.

Thought is the Cause. The outcome of that thought is the Effect … provided that the person doing the thinking also invests the necessary effort/work into creating those results. Or, as Thomas Troward suggested in The Edinburgh Lectures on Mental Science (1904), "the action of Mind plants that nucleus which, if allowed to grow undisturbed, will eventually attract to itself all the conditions necessary for its manifestation in outward visible form."

Some scientists claim that the Law of Attraction in medical applications is an example of the placebo effect. The placebo effect is a simulated medical intervention that can produce (perceived or actual) improvement.

Research has shown clinical improvement for a variety of medical problems in patients treated with a placebo. This has been proven to be the case even when the patient KNEW s/he had been given the placebo!

Several researchers have found that a placebo is 50% as effective as any analgesic, including morphine. Further, researchers have found that placebos can actually reverse the action of potent drugs. The effectiveness of placebo treatment can be interpreted as compelling evidence that expectation and belief can affect physiological response.

Recent studies using spectral analysis and topographic electroencephalographic (EEG) mapping of the relaxation response demonstrate that by changing mental activity, we can demonstrate measurable changes in central nervous system activity. These, and other, studies demonstrate that mind–body interactions are real and can be measured.

So, let's examine that claim that the Law of Attraction in medical applications might be an example of the placebo effect.  The placebo effect might suggest that I experienced a healing result because I believed I was given the effective medication/combination-of-remedies that would create the healing.

Now, if, indeed, my belief that – with the proper combination of remedies – I could be arthritis-free set up the conditions for such a positive placebo-effect-result on a Universal level, I think this is great!  Or, if my mind was so powerful that it could take a "simulated medical intervention" and use it to direct my body to create an effective cure from arthritis, I think this is great!  Or, if there is some other combination of operant principles active, I think this, too, is great!

Whichever way it may be – in my opinion and experience, this proves the point about Universal Principle and subconscious-mind creativity:  That which we firmly claim as our reality is creative … creative of exactly that outcome!  My response is "I'll take it!" … and feel hugely blessed!

# PART III:    MY PERSONAL JOURNEY
## SECTION III:  TAKING THE STEPS

### Chapter 3:  Specific Steps to Healing – Physical-Mental

**Step #8 – Exercise (pre-1968)**

Exercise is any form of physical activity that enhances or maintains physical fitness and overall health and wellness. Exercise can take on many forms and is performed for various reasons.

Reasons for exercising can include enjoyment, strengthening muscles and the cardiovascular system, honing athletic skills, and weight loss/maintenance. Frequent and regular physical exercise boosts the immune system, and helps prevent the "diseases of affluence" such as heart disease, cardiovascular disease, Type 2 diabetes, and obesity. It also improves mental health, helps prevent and reduce depression, helps to increase positive self-esteem, and augments an individual's sex appeal or body image.

From the time I was a teenager, I had engaged in regular physical activity and routine exercise.  After developing rheumatoid arthritis, I found that I felt much, much better when I exercised.  Hence, I renewed my dedication to adhering to exercise as an everyday practice.

Not only did exercise help my physical flexibility and muscle strength, it relieved major portions of joint stiffness.  In addition, daily exercise also kept my mood up and my mind focused in positive directions. It was commonplace to see me down on the floor – stretching, doing non-weighted repetitions, engaging in physical strengthening, doing yoga poses, etc.

Another benefit for me was that, once I had rid myself of arthritis, I had a habit of being physically fit and flexible. Hence, continuing exercise and physical activity as a lifestyle-choice has been easy for me to do. Doing so has served to reinforce and deepen the ongoing healing response that I still experience.

# PART III:   MY PERSONAL JOURNEY
## SECTION III:  TAKING THE STEPS

### Chapter 4:  Specific Steps to Healing – Mental-Emotional

#### Step #9 -- Thoughts => Feelings (1976)

Thoughts affect feelings.  This is a major tenet of Cognitive and Cognitive-Behavioral belief-systems in psychology.

How we choose to think has a direct effect on how we feel. This matters because we can start to become aware of our thought and – if we find that we are thinking counterproductively to the experience we want to have – we can CHANGE the thought!  Changing the thought creates a reciprocal change in the feeling that was an outgrowth of the original thought.

So, I can choose to affect my emotional responding in situations where a previously-learned emotional response might be ineffective.  The way I would do this is by – first, changing my thought – and letting that change create the corresponding outcome in the area of my feeling.

So, if I find that a certain way of feeling – let's say, feeling angry – makes my condition worse, I can begin to change the way I mentally process the situation that led me to feel anger, originally.  For example, I can mentally process the situation and reach a state in which I feel more peaceful about that situation.  Or, I could mentally process the situation so as to release feelings of hurt, etc., which might have been fundamental to the original anger.

There are many choices I can make … IF I recognize what is occurring within me and know to make different choices. If I just go on "automatic pilot", I can be in the middle of a damaging, destructive outburst and never know how I got there!

I found my experience of rheumatoid arthritis to be very responsive to my emotions. When I was impatient, I tensed up and was in more pain. When I was angry, I developed more pain.

When I was feeling tense and stressed, my joints reflected this with more stiffness and tightness. When I felt overwhelmed, my joints responded to this, making me unable to move.

Learning constructive ways to release emotion was important to reducing my body's arthritic results. Learning cognitive processing strategies to eliminate (not deny) the emotional responding was important to reducing my body's arthritic responding.

In addition, examining my mental processing and creating more-effective mental processes were important steps to reducing my body's arthritic outcomes.

Needless to say, my pursuit of Psychology allowed me vital learning regarding these new patterns of responding. This was – definitely – a fortuitous choice of educational direction! In essence, I had a resident Psychologist with skills and expertise to help me change old patterns … and develop new, effective ways to handle my life and myself.

## Step #10 -- Acceptance and Self-care (1977)

Throughout my years of education in Psychology and my involvement in the profession, I learned more about the importance of self-acceptance and loving oneself. Without a doubt, both of these are important emotional needs! However, I find that, in general, in most people's lives, they are too often overlooked.

Acceptance is the agreement to experience something as it is, without trying to change it. Self-acceptance refers to experiencing oneself, just as one is, without trying to change oneself. Self-acceptance includes self-understanding and a lack of criticism and judgment.

In accepting yourself just as you are, it does NOT mean that you never change. Quite on the contrary! In accepting yourself just as you are, you free up valuable energy – energy that, otherwise, is consumed in non-acceptance. It requires a HUGE amount of energy to not accept oneself.

Well, when you accept yourself, all of that energy is liberated. It is, then, at your disposal to direct specifically to those areas in which you most desire to have change. So, you have this massive amount of energy to facilitate the very change(s) that you would like to make.

Then, you accept yourself at each step in the process of making the desired change. You also accept the "you" that you become, as a result of completing the desired change.

In the course of my healing quest, I found that accepting myself fully just as I am/was also paved the way to loving myself just as I am/was. Once I was treating myself consistently with love, it became easy to accomplish those tasks that showed myself the most care.

Taking good care of myself required self-knowledge and self-awareness. To care for myself in a loving way, I – first – had to know what I needed. Then, and only then, could I set forth to meet those needs and take good care of me!

In my experience, healing required a complete dedication to the steps of acceptance – not criticism and judgment – and self-care. It required – at a very-basic and yet quite-consuming level – that I bestow intense self-care energy and time on myself and my healing … with the absolute knowing that I was WORTH every joule and minute of it!

## Step #11 – Hypnotherapy for Mental Clearing (1978)

I first learned Hypnosis in 1978. It was the answer to a search that I had undertaken to learn a more-effective way to assist clients in their process to change. I wanted a tool that I could use – and that I could teach to my clients – that would be simple and successful! Hypnosis, self-hypnosis and hypnotherapy have, certainly, turned out to be for me the answers to that request.

Hypnosis is a state of consciousness – a state of mind – in which the subject is physically relaxed, with his/her mind alert and aware. In the state of hypnosis, the subconscious mind becomes more accessible. In the state of hypnosis, the subconscious mind becomes highly suggestible to positive ideas and to releasing barriers from the past.

Hypnosis is powerful, simple, quick, and effective. It gets results ... in a subtle, intense, incredibly effective way.

My introduction to Hypnosis occurred as a result of a couple of unplanned (by me!) scenarios. In the first, I was working with an extremely-anxious client. His fear and nervous-upset were so great that they got in the way of treatment.

So, I decided to introduce him to systematized relaxation. As I was guiding him through the relaxation exercise, he spontaneously regressed to being 3 years old, involved in an emotional situation that had severely traumatized him.

This occurrence certainly surprised me! However, I had long been a believer that whatever happened during therapy was part of the treatment process, so I said to myself, "Let's work with this." And we did – with the outcome that he released the long-ago trauma and was able from then on to conduct his life without the anxiety that had previously kept him imprisoned and his life restricted.

My inner responses were, "Wow! That was powerful" and "What just happened?"

I resolved to learn more ...

At about this very same time, I had another client who had intense life-long issues. He said to me, "I want to use Hypnosis to work on this." It's my belief that clients often know what will work best for them. In this regard, I believe that it is my task to help them "get in touch" with their own inner wisdom. I responded, "OK, then, if that's what you believe will work best, I encourage you to do that. However, I am not a Hypnotist so I won't be able to help you with it."

My client was very patient with me. He said, "No, I want you to go with me to a Hypnotist, let the Hypnotist hypnotize me and, then, transfer the control to you and have you do the therapy within the Hypnosis." This latter approach – doing therapy with the client in the Hypnotic state is a well-regarded procedure known as "Hypnotherapy". (Of course, I did not know this at the time; I only learned it later.) However, his proposal sounded intriguing to me.

And that is what we did. We went to his Hypnotist and, while the Hypnotist was hypnotizing this client, I got my answer to what had happened with my previous client. That first client had gone into a spontaneous Hypnotic trance! Needless to say, I was "hooked" and had to learn more, especially about specific, focused, intentional ways to USE this powerful technique!

I started Hypnosis classes that next weekend!

In addition to learning how to Hypnotize clients, I also learned self-Hypnosis. Using this technique, I was able to not only create a quick method of self-relaxation and access to the depths of my subconscious mind, I was also able to probe that part of my mind about the Arthritis.

In the process of diligent and repeated self-Hypnosis, I uncovered a series of faulty beliefs that pre-dated the time when I experienced my first symptoms of arthritis.

These beliefs were total misunderstandings about my own nature and my relation to the Universe. Discovering these ideas was profound! Discovering these ideas turned out to be a true ah-ha! moment for me. Once I uncovered the faulty beliefs, right away I intuitively KNEW, "Of course! that can't possibly be true!"

This mental discovery created an incredible, instantaneous, corresponding emotional release. In addition, this discovery paved the way to allowing my body to release the physical illness-pattern that it had – mistakenly – taken on as a direct result of those faulty beliefs.

As I mentioned above, at this point, I also applied forgiveness. I forgave myself for the false beliefs that I'd had. I forgave myself for believing something so damaging. I forgave myself for thinking that I needed to have such ideas. This forgiveness completed my release … and prepared the way for the Physical Steps to Healing (Steps #14, #15, and #16) to work so incredibly well.

*Iron rusts from disuse; stagnant water loses*

*its purity and in cold weather becomes frozen;*

*even so does inaction sap the vigor of the mind.*

-- Leonardo da Vinci

# PART III: MY PERSONAL JOURNEY
## SECTION III: TAKING THE STEPS

### Chapter 5: Specific Steps to Healing – Mental-Physical

**Step #12 – Breathing (1960-1977)**

Beginning with Meditation – and following through with other modalities that I progressively learned in my healing quest, not the least of which is Hypnosis – I discovered the importance of effective breathing. What I found is that breathing is VITALLY important for life and health, as well as for mental-emotional well-being.

I discovered that, to get the maximum effects from breathing, it is important to breathe deeply, rhythmically, evenly, and slowly. It is important to make this type of breathing a habit.

Let me explain why this is the case …

Deep, slow, rhythmic breathing is the pathway --
a) to effective stress relief
b) for a clearer mind
c) for release of frustration and irritation
    -- release the negative emotion along with the air each
       time you exhale
d) for relaxation
e) to deeper, more restful sleep
f) for an easier time falling asleep and staying asleep
g) to create inner calm and peace
h) for complete and speedy healing and recovery
i) to energize your body and your whole being

Amazingly enough, breathing is the one physiological process that normally proceeds non-consciously. However, it is a physiological process that can be consciously controlled ... if one pays attention to do so.

Here's what I discovered to be the reason why effective breathing matters so profoundly ...

Every cell of your body needs oxygen. It needs oxygen to stay strong and healthy. It needs oxygen to heal, should something get out of balance. You can usually go several hours without having fluids and be OK. You can go a month without food (not that I'm suggesting that you do so!) and still be OK. You cannot go 5 minutes without breathing ... without serious repercussions and brain damage.

When you do not breathe deeply and fully, your body -- subtly -- begins to tense up. It does this because it knows that it is being put into jeopardy. If you breathe shallowly or hold your breath, you are setting the stage for your body to become very tense.

In addition, notice your own breathing patterns. What happens when you begin to get tense? If you are like most people, you start to let your breathing go shallow and quick. What happens if you have a shock? If you are like most people, you intake breath rapidly then hold it. In other words, you STOP breathing. Since breathing is SO essential to human well-being -- and very life -- the LAST thing you would want to do is inhibit your deep, full pattern of breathing.

I found that the solution is simple!

What I needed to do is focus on a slow, deep exhale. A slow count of 4 worked very well for me for this. Then, I would pause a second. Next, I'd inhale with a slow, deep breath to the slow count of 4. Then, I would pause again a second ... and repeat the process.

Oxygen is the matter of life. Giving myself plenty of oxygen allows all of my being -- physical, mental, emotional and spiritual -- to function more effectively. Giving myself plenty of oxygen naturally allows stress to be released and relaxation to be increased. It allows my whole being to receive vital energy. Breathing out fully, then breathing in fully allows me to energize, to take in life!

To effectively rid myself of rheumatoid arthritis took an abundance of the life-giving substance, oxygen. There was MUCH in my physical body that required oxygen for healing. Allowing myself to create a habit of de-stressing – a habit of relaxation – not only promoted my healing, but also required plenty of oxygen!

## Step #13 – Relaxation (1978)

I discovered that relaxation was an essential step to allow my body to heal. The physical body does its best healing during sleep. It does its next-best healing while at rest. As was mentioned above, I found the habit of breathing deeply and slowly to be a vital component of relaxation – especially of the type of relaxation that created my best healing response.

The understanding of the physiology of mind-body interactions – and the importance of relaxation and other methods to reduce stress – was advanced in the 1950s by studies conducted by Walter Hess and by Hans Selye. Hess (*The Functional Organization of the Diencephalon*. New York: Grune & Stratton, 1957: 35-44) documented both the body's emergency reaction to stress and the response known as the "relaxation response". Hans Selye (*The Stress of Life*. New York: McCraw Hill, 1956: 118-224) studied the neuroendocrine effects of the fight-or-flight response and the resulting General Adaptation Syndrome.

The three (3) phases of the General Adaptation Syndrome are the Alarm Stage, the Resistance Stage, and the Exhaustion Stage. In the Alarm Stage, the body shows a stress reaction – the body gives the message that it is not dealing well with stress. In the Resistance Stage, the body works hard to restore equilibrium; it gives its owner time to reduce sustained stress and lower the overall level of existent stress.

If stress is not reduced, Selye described that the body progresses to the Third Stage. Dr. Selye demonstrated that the third phase -- the Exhaustion Phase – could result in illness and, even, ultimately, death. Dr. Selye discussed the importance to effectively counter those effects of stress to prevent such an ultimate occurrence as illness and death. Yes! Selye definitely showed that stress could kill!

In contrast, Dr. Hans Selye discussed the fact that successful stress relief was needed to influence vitality and good health! He saw effective stress management as a necessity to reverse the progression in the body's reaction to stress in what he termed the General Adaptation Syndrome.

# PART III:   MY PERSONAL JOURNEY
## SECTION III:  TAKING THE STEPS

### Chapter 6:  Specific Steps to Healing – Physical

**Step #14 -- Hair Analysis => Vitamin and Mineral
                        Supplementation (1979)**

One evening, I was talking with a chiropractor-friend.  During our discussion, he was inspired to suggest that we do a hair analysis on me.  He speculated that there might be a nutritional basis for the arthritis that I'd had so long.  To find out, he clipped my hair and sent it to the laboratory.

A hair analysis is a test of a hair sample to determine if there are any vitamin-or-mineral deficiencies – or any heavy metal toxicities – present inside a person.  The theory is that the hair would absorb the heavy metal and reveal its presence; at the same time, it would show a representative level of vitamins and minerals in the body.  While this procedure is controversial for some in the medical profession, it certainly worked for me.

When the results of this test came back, the report classified me as a slow oxidizer.  It indicated that I was in need of a serious regimen of vitamins and minerals, in specific proportions.  It also defined specific alterations in my food habits/diet.

These recommendations were extensive.  They required that I take at least 40 vitamin and mineral tablets a day.  It also directed me to reduce my food choices primarily to fresh vegetables and fruits, chicken, fish and nuts, and moderate amounts of dairy products.

Just preparing each day's vitamin-mineral dosage took almost ten minutes in itself, apportioning them into their respective baggies! I realized that to follow this program would require a dedicated commitment on my part. For me, it really came down to just that: If I were going to do it, I would do it all. Otherwise, I would do none of it.

I decided to do it all. What, really, did I have to lose? Exactly!!

Despite my absolute dedication to this dietary/vitamin mineral regimen, I saw no results during the first month. At the end of this time, I reassessed my commitment. Was it really worth all the time, energy, and conscientious focus that I was putting into it?

Even though I admit to being somewhat discouraged and disappointed at the lack of any results during this period of time, I decided to go ahead with the program. After all, I had had arthritis for 13+ years by this time. Certainly, it made complete sense to me that what I had dealt with for all that time just might not disappear in 30 days!

Another month came and went with me adhering religiously to the treatment plan. Still, I saw no results. In addition to the vitamins and minerals, I was still on all the arthritis medications. I still had constant, unrelenting pain, severe distress, and ongoing infirmity. I continued my regular schedule of consistent exercise at a health club, teaching two community-college classes (6 credit hours), and counseling psychotherapy clients.

Once again, I decided to continue the hair analysis program for a while longer ... and awhile longer ... and awhile longer until, soon, six months had passed. To my growing bemusement, I still had seen no overt physical results. However, during these six months, an interesting phenomenon had occurred. I had become more and more certain that something WAS happening within my body. I felt as though I were "setting the stage" for results that were still to come.

So, I turned my search in other directions.

## Step #15 -- Edgar Cayce Remedies (1980)

But where to search?

Quite frankly, I had not the slightest idea! However, I made my request of the Universe: remember – the prayer, affirmations, and Meditation? Through these practices, I asked that the next step present itself.

And so it did.

When I first moved to Phoenix in 1968, my roommate told me about Edgar Cayce and the A.R.E. Clinic (the Associations for Research and Enlightenment – with clinic offices in Virginia Beach, VA, and in Phoenix, AZ). I found this information interesting – even intriguing – and I did extensive research on it. However, I did not pursue it further at that time.

This quickly changed once I had requested that my next step be made clear to me. The next step presented itself in the form of a question posed to me by still another friend (Where would I be without my friends? I never want to find out!). This friend knew of my growing preference for holistic approaches to physical health and healing.

One day, I was describing to him the healing approach of Edgar Cayce and the programs at the A.R.E. Clinic. I had been quite animated describing what-I-found-to-be quite an exciting approach. It had been quite a lively conversation. Once I finished, my friend asked me a simple question: "Why don't you go there?" – referring the A.R.E. Clinic in Phoenix.

It seemed like such an obvious choice. Yet, despite the fact that I had suggested it to others numerous times in the past, I had not thought of it for myself!! How nice that someone else helped me out!

I felt an immediate KNOWING that this was a perfect answer for me. Without delay, I called the A.R.E. Clinic. The Clinic was well known to have a massive, months'-long waiting list. When I called, I was pleasantly surprised to find out that an appointment was available with one of the two head physicians – William McGarey, M.D. – the very next week.

I took it!

Dr. Bill is a kindly, soft-spoken man with a wealth of experience in the fields of medicine and healing. He practices – and the A.R.E. Clinic (which used to be here, in Phoenix) was dedicated to advancing – the treatments prescribed by the outstanding psychic and mystic Edgar Cayce (*Dreams: Your Magic Mirror, Seers out of Season, Mysteries of the Mind*).

When he died in 1945 at the age of 67, Cayce left behind a rich legacy of more than 14,000 readings. In his practice, Cayce would go into a self-induced trance and psychically access information regarding appropriate physical/mental/ emotional treatment for the specific condition that a patient happened to present to him. His readings continue to be researched and utilized in medical practice today.

The information that Cayce revealed described man as an eternal, spiritual being, with creative powers of the mind. He explained that man's mind – working with spiritual energy – creates the body which man utilizes in this physical dimension. Hence, the mind in conjunction with the body's own wisdom can create a healed, whole physical body. This body can then fulfill its mission to maintain life, unimpeded. Operating in this fashion, the body enables humans to actively attain the destiny and purpose of their existence.

Dr. Bill relayed that Cayce utilized a basic approach. Edgar Cayce felt that if a coordination of the bodily functions of respiration, circulation, assimilation, elimination, and regeneration could be achieved, healing was inevitable.

As the doctor explained it, Cayce's view encompassed a therapy designed to balance and bring into attunement the functioning body; the mind – with its emotions, attitudes and beliefs; and the spiritual reality. In most cases, it was this harmony that resulted in good physical health.

Next, Dr. Bill (*The Edgar Cayce Remedies*, 1983) discussed with me Cayce's view on the causes of arthritis. He recounted that the sources of arthritis as researched in the Cayce readings were limited to seven categories: poor assimilation and elimination, impaired circulation, glandular malfunction, karmic and psychological causes, previous treatments, spinal subluxations, and injuries.

He explained to me that poor elimination, and its associated and resultant condition – inadequate assimilation, which causes improper lymph function – seemed to be a part of the picture for Cayce in nearly every condition of arthritis, no matter what type it may be. This begins with the production of excess stomach acid, a condition often triggered by stress-related emotions. Dr Bill described that the improper elimination leads to a buildup of toxins within the body. This, in turn, would eventually lead to such a strain on the systems that an arthritic condition resulted.

Then, the doctor added that, according to Cayce, glandular incoordination was also a major factor in the cause of arthritis. The lack of proper hormone secretions appeared to contribute to problems with the circulation, blood and calcium levels, and the absorption of minerals from food.

Dr. Bill described to me that Cayce's approach sought to re-establish the essential balance in the body. Cayce

110

explained this, by saying, "The causes or sources of these conditions are of a very subtle nature. The effects that have been produced in the extremities are hard to cope with." He described that results would occur through the use of consistency and persistence in using the suggestions that he gave. The treatments that were to be followed would "first meet the conditions, gradually cleanse the system, and then begin to renew the energies of the body." (3244-1; from the Cayce readings)

Next, I was instructed in the importance of following the practice to apply the therapy in cycles. It was pointed out that each Cayce-reading-given-for-arthritis used the cyclic nature of treatment. Throughout treatment, it was important that the doctor watch the balance of my body as a whole.

With these comments as baseline, I was given the following four-item therapeutic approach:

1. Assimilations – including diet and control of digestive abnormalities.

2. Eliminations – this might be done with castor oil packs, various eliminants, colonics, and enemas. It would also include hydrotherapy, such as normal hot baths and Epsom salts baths.

3. Massage – used to improve the nerve-supply to the muscles and tendons, and those coordinating the various organs. Various oils and mixtures were given in the readings, some irritating in nature and others soothing in nature.

4. Stimulate normal glandular functions – this would be done through the use of Atomic Iodine, a substance called Atomidine. Atomidine, a fluid with high iodine content for stimulating the thyroid gland, was to be taken only in specific cycles under a physician's supervision. Cayce warned that excess iodine in the system could over-stimulate the thyroid gland and result in harmful effects on the body.

Next, Dr. Bill reviewed for me the specific treatment that he advocated that I follow. This was directly based on the readings that Cayce specified for healing arthritis. Cayce's treatment focused on restoring the body's capacity to function normally, thereby stimulating the system's natural efforts to heal itself. Secondary to this were methods of relieving pain; Cayce viewed these as merely symptoms of the illness, not its causes.

The steps that were outlined for me included:

1. Atomic Iodine: Atomidine – one drop in half a glass of water daily before breakfast, for the first day; two drops in half a glass of water for the second day; three drops for the third day; four drops for the fourth day; then five drops on the fifth day.

2. For each of the next three days, I was to take an Epsom salts bath (to stimulate circulation) with 15 pounds of salts to 50 gallons of water. The water was to be hot as I could stand it. I was to soak in it for twenty to thirty minutes.

3. A peanut-oil rubdown massage was to be used immediately after I had dried off from the Epsom-salt bath. This was to take advantage of the pores being maximally open, as a result of the bath.

4. During these three days, I was to focus most intensely on rest.

5. Then I was directed to start the Atomidine cycle again. This was to be followed by the cycle of Epsom-salts baths, full-body massages, and rest.

6. Twice each day – morning and night, I was to massage the affected joints with a pine-oil based massage oil. Massage was to be given in a firm, gentle, rotary motion. Its purpose was to stimulation circulation, to relieve pain and discomfort, and to assist the body in removing toxic substances.

7. Each evening, I was to use castor-oil packs (http://www.cayce.com/castoroil.htm) for thirty minutes placed on the abdomen and for an additional thirty minutes on the joints that were most affected. A dry-heat heating pad was used over the packs. The heated castor oil pack procedure stimulated the elimination of toxic substances from my body and helped restore equilibrium to my digestion and elimination.

8. To eliminate toxins, I was to use enemas or colonics. In the beginning, these were to be taken every third day. After a few weeks, this was extended to once a week for a couple of months; then, as needed. I found it interesting that this

treatment was not designed to correct the original causes of the imbalances; it was to cleanse my intestines, thereby reducing irritation and pressure.

9. Diet was to include no fried foods; meat could be fish, fowl, and lamb; juices were good, especially vegetable juices; cooked beets and carrots were especially good; no carbonated drinks. See more specifics about diet, below.

10. I was advised to exercise as much as possible. For Cayce, exercise was seen as a great rejuvenator – both on the physical and the mental-emotional planes. He saw it as vital in reducing the stiffness and restriction in motion that is prevalent in the vast majority of arthritics. It was to be conducted regularly and in moderation. Cayce believed that a system already under stress needed to be gently led to the experience of ease, not overtaxed by too much physical activity. Lucky me – I already had a solid habit of exercise. I had made this into a daily discipline once I recognized how much better I felt as a result.

11. Also recommended was spinal manipulation, a system of therapy to manually manipulate the vertebrae of the spinal column. Dr. Bill explained that Cayce noted that general manipulation served to facilitate natural adjustments by breaking up congested areas and helping ganglia under strain adjust so that both proper drainage and stimulated circulation to the organs would occur. These manipulations could be of the disciplines of osteopathy, chiropractic or neuropathy.

12.  In addition, Edgar Cayce advocated proper attitudes and emotions. According to Cayce's prescribed remedies, cultivating a mental attitude conducive to healing was essential!  Cayce believed that positive thinking prevented further consequences from emotional stress.  It opened the body-mind to the Source of all healing – which is spiritual and creative in nature.

Dr. Bill told me that Cayce reminded those seeking physical relief that the "mind is the builder" of health, as well as of illness.  He described it as a demonstration of faith, for instance, to be "consistent and persistent" with treatments.

Undoubtedly, the most consistent routine of therapy for arthritis in the Cayce readings was the combination of Atomic Iodine, Epsom salts baths, and massage.  This theme is played over and over again with varying periods of time allotted to the administration of Atomidine; with varying amounts of Epsom salts in the hot bath; and with different varieties of oils used for massage.  This regimen was for the purpose of providing glandular stimulation.

Dr. Bill directed that I repeat these therapeutic measures in cycles – with rest periods between – until my body returned to normal. I was to remain mindful of the condition of my whole body, of course, and the assimilation and eliminations were to be made as proper as possible.

## Step #16 -- Healthy Food Selection:  Diet & Food Recommendations (1980)

Dr. Bill was clear that diet assumed a major proportion in the treatment for arthritis as found in the readings.  It seemed to be understood if not stated, that the diet be of a laxative nature.

Next, Dr. Bill described that Edgar Cayce emphasized the importance of maintaining a proper acid-alkaline balance by eating mostly alkaline-forming foods.  According to the Cayce-recommendations, a typical diet for arthritic individuals placed emphasis on alkaline-forming foods – 80% of my daily diet was to contain these foods:

* All kinds of raw vegetables except tomatoes, cabbage, dried beans, lentils, asparagus tips, and garbanzos; these may be eaten with Knox gelatin  (Gelatin was seen as a catalyst in the body, helping it make use of the vitamins and other properties of vegetables and fruits)
* All fresh fruits except strawberries, apples, cranberries, plums, olives, prunes, and blueberries (preserves and canned fruits are usually acid-forming)
* Whole grains – pumpernickel, rye, whole wheat, black bread
* Almonds (especially), chestnuts, Brazil nuts, and hazelnuts
* Light proteins – fish and seafood, fowl, lamb, wild game, and liver
* Vegetable juices, citrus fruit juices at times when cereal was not eaten.

\* Cooked leafy vegetables (except cabbage); oyster plant (salsify); parsnips; potato peelings from the baked potato, but not the bulk of it.

Foods to be avoided were
-- white flour and its products; white potatoes (except their skins)
-- fried foods
-- carbonated drinks and alcohol
-- fruits – apples, bananas, strawberries, tomatoes
-- red meat (beef or veal)

Combinations of foods to be avoided were
-- starches and sugar at the same meal
-- coffee or tea with milk or cream, and
-- citrus fruits or juices with cereals or dairy products

Attitudes & Emotions for Eating: Edgar Cayce stated that even the most nutritious foods could turn to poison in the system if eaten while a person is in a negative frame of mind. He advocated to never eat when angry, worried or extremely tired.

Interestingly enough(!), the diet recommendations that I had already been using in conjunction with the results of the hair analysis were totally consistent with the Cayce diet suggestions. So, the very patterns of eating which I had been using for the past 6 months, continued to serve me well as I undertook this multi-faceted, time-and-energy demanding regimen.

*Everything has beauty,*

*But not everyone sees it.*

-- Confucius

# PART III: MY PERSONAL JOURNEY
## SECTION III: TAKING THE STEPS

### Chapter 7: Specific Steps to Healing – The Results

Once again, as I did when I undertook the vitamin-mineral regimen 6 months earlier, I decided that, since I was serious about wanting to be rid of Arthritis, I needed to make a serious decision. I determined that I needed to diligently follow each and every one of the steps outlined by Dr. Bill. Following the recommendations of Edgar Cayce, explained to me by Dr. Bill McGarey would take a minimum of 1 – 2 hours per day. To me, that was a LOT of time!

I decided that – if it had a chance to work – that chance rested in my willingness to follow each and every step, each and every day. It was just that discipline that I dedicated myself to accomplish.

And the Results were quick in coming!

At the time that I started the Edgar Cayce remedies, I was getting injections of gold salts every 10 days. I was taking 24 aspirin a day. I was on daily prednisone. I was taking phenaphen #3 (with codeine) and percodan every 4 hours for pain. And I was in full-fledged, massively active arthritis – with frequent flare-ups, and constant pain.

In the first few days of following through with Edgar Cayce's recommendations, I saw a difference. I never again needed – or received – an injection of gold salts! I started feeling better … more flexible … less stiffness and joint pain … almost from Day 1!

Never being one who would pause at stretching the envelope, I then tried to cut back on prednisone. I was very careful … I only tried to cut down by ¼ a tablet once every two days.

Mistake!

Immediately I experienced a recurrence of the joint swelling, stiffness, and pain. Everything became worse once again! So, I went right back on my usual prednisone dosage.

Undeterred, though, I started to reduce my dosage of aspirin. I began to cut back by 1 every week. So, by the end of week 1, I was taking 11 aspirin a day. By the end of week 2, I was taking 10 aspirin a day. By the end of 12 weeks, I was totally off from the aspirin!

During this time, since I was feeling so incredibly good – with vastly reduced pain and stiffness and joint swelling – I started to reduce the phenaphen and percodan and, over these same 3 months, I had completely eliminated all of these pain medications

Then, I undertook my hardest challenge: to get off prednisone. Needless to say, after my earlier foray in this direction, I was apprehensive. However, I was feeling so much better that I KNEW it was time that I complete the process.

So, I gathered up my courage – continued to breathe and stay relaxed – and started to reduce the dosage of prednisone. I cut back by 1/4 tablet, every 2 days. Now – that was a "trick", considering that the tablets were very, very tiny to start with! I persisted – and at the end of those first 2 weeks, rather than having taken 14 tablets, I had taken 12 ½ tablets. In that 2 weeks, I had cut back by 1 ½ tablets, total! Now, while that might not seem like a lot, it represented a MAJOR breakthrough for me!

Not much of a reduction, you might be thinking. And, while that was true, the Good News was that I did not experience regression to my prior levels of pain, stiffness, swelling or disability. I was ecstatic!

Then, for the next 2 weeks, I took ¼ tablet less each day. So, after the first month of prednisone reduction, rather than having taken 14 tablets, I had taken 11 tablets.

Then, for the next 2 weeks, I reduced my dosage by ½ tablet every other day. So, in the next 2 weeks, rather than having taken 14 tablets, I actually took 7 tablets. I had reduced my dosage by ½ in 2 months.

Then, I continued with this rate of reduction for the next 2 months. At that time, I was totally off from prednisone … after 14 years! So, within 7 months of starting the Edgar Cayce remedies, I was off all medication … AND experiencing NO pain, NO stiffness, NO joint swelling … NO arthritis!

I am delighted to report that this continued to be the case for the next 30 years!

*Victory belongs to the most persevering.*

-- Napoleon Bonaparte

# PART III: MY PERSONAL JOURNEY
## SECTION III: TAKING THE STEPS

### Chapter 8: Specific Steps to Healing – Your Turn

It is this precise point that has been my goal throughout the process of writing of this book. This juncture is the reason I undertook to write this book. I already knew what had worked so incredibly well. I didn't need to put it on paper.

I wrote this book for you, my reader. More specifically, I wrote this book especially for you, my reader with arthritis. It is my goal to make it possible for you to duplicate – or surpass – my success! After knowing from personal experience the daily misery of living with chronic pain and infirmity, I have enjoyed each day of being pain-free for the past 30 years. I feel driven to pass this information on to as many people as are willing to follow the steps that worked for me and reap comparable rewards!

It is my pleasure to outline for you how you, too, can follow the Program that worked for me. Here are the steps that I would take, if I were starting out today. Here's how you can do what I did ... and how to make it work for yourself!:

A. Make a **Firm Commitment to Yourself**: Decide that you are Worth It!

  1. Decide that Your Good Health is worth whatever it takes to secure it

2. Commit to this Program FULLY
   -- get clear in your mind to follow-through on each step
   -- resolve complete each step fully, each day
   -- get clear in your mind that there will be no "half measures"

3. Determine that You value Yourself – and love Yourself – so much that you feel privileged to care for Yourself in the ways described below.

4. Would you like help to build strong self esteem and value yourself this highly? For specific step-by-step direction to build self esteem, visit:
   **http://2affirm.com/esteem.htm**

B. Start a Daily Program: Begin daily sessions of
   **1. Exercise**
   For Cayce, exercise was a source of physical and mental-emotional rejuvenation. Used regularly and in moderation, it reduces the stiffness and restriction-in-motion common to arthritics. Since the arthritic system is already under serious stress, Cayce theorized that exercise needs to be moderate – so that it does not overtax the system, but, rather, that it serves to gently lead the system into a state of ease.
   a. Discuss exercise with your physician. Use her/his advice on how you can best begin;
   b. In general, begin slowly – perhaps, with just 5' -10'; then, gradually, work your way up to 30' each day.
   c. If possible, choose activities that you enjoy. When you do this, it makes it more probable that you will follow-through consistently.

d.Then, talk yourself INTO exercising.  Many times, people decide to do something and, then, proceed to tell themselves all of the reasons NOT to do it.  For example, "I'm too tired" or "I'll go tomorrow" or "It's too late".  In essence, this talks you OUT of exercising.  On the other hand, when you tell yourself, "I can't wait to exercise!" or "It will feel so good once I'm moving my body!" – you talk yourself INTO the action.

e.Schedule the time for exercise and put it into your planner each day.  Then, when that time comes up, you won't have anything else filling that space and, as a result, it will be easier to start the positive self-messages talking yourself into getting active!

## 2. Meditation

a. Schedule the time for meditation – at least 20' – 30' each day.  Select a specific time – and use the same time each day.  Put this time into your day-planner and follow your schedule consistently.

b. There are many different techniques of meditation.  Select a method that appeals to you and begin consistent sessions for yourself.

c . Are you interested in pre-recorded meditations?  For a variety of focused meditations, visit:
**http://thelifecoachdr.com/coach/meditation**
Here, you will find meditations on many different topics for your use.

d. Below is a simple meditation-format to get you started:

## Meditation:  Basic Mindfulness

Create a quiet place. Sit comfortably. Allow both of your feet to touch the ground. Your arms may rest on the chair. Permit your hands to rest in your lap. Close your eyes.

Pause a moment to clear your mind -- anything that has occurred earlier in the day, let it go.  Anything that might be occurring later, let it go.  Any cares, any burdens – let the go. Focus your attention on this present moment ... This is the only moment that any of us have.  This moment is all there is.

Now, in this present moment, start to be aware of your breathing.  Notice each breath -- as you exhale, as you inhale.  If your mind wanders, just gently -- firmly -- bring it back to pay attention to your breathing.

Exhale ...

Inhale...

Allow each exhalation -- each inhalation -- to be slower, longer. Allow there to be a slight pause after each exhalation before beginning the next inhalation.  Then, pause as well after each inhalation before beginning the next exhalation.

Slowly... longer ... deeper ...

Exhale ...

Inhale...

Your body will sink deeper into the chair. As you relax, your body will feel heavier and very still.

Exhale ...

Inhale...

If your mind begins to wander, return to consciously paying attention to your breathing.

You will gradually start to become aware that your mind is starting to clear. There is no busy clutter to interfere with your ability to relax. Quietness envelops you.

Exhale ...

Inhale...

Continue this through your 20' - 30' period. Some days it will be as long as half an hour. On other days, it may only twenty minutes. Whichever it may be, you will feel refreshed from the brief pause.

As you end your meditation, you will feel yourself almost awakening. Pause.

Sit still a moment. Take several deep, slow breaths and return to whatever activity awaits you. You are now ready to move around a hand or a foot, then slowly stand and begin to move around.

During your day, pause for a moment to remember how good you felt during your meditation. When you do this, you begin to automatically return to that mind-body sense of peace. In this way, you can touch it with your mind whenever you need to.

Use this meditation every day. Doing so, will allow you to begin to experience deeper and deeper meditation.

### 3. Relaxation

To create enhanced stress reduction, begin to notice your breathing throughout the day. Specifically, notice when you start to change the rhythm of your breathing from slow and deep. This is important: Catch this when it just begins to change. This is the most beneficial time to bring it back to a regular rhythm that is deep and slow.

### Relaxation: Breathing Basics:

a. Make a habit to notice your breathing pattern: for effective breathing, you want a pattern that is deep and slow and regular;

b. If you notice that you are breathing irregularly, take the time to alter your breathing to a pattern that is slow, deep and regular;

c. Begin to take Breathing Breaks: Every hour, make it a habit to take 15 slow, deep breaths; during this time, allow yourself to relax fully and completely. Focus on exhaling first ... 1 - 2 - 3 - 4 ... pause ... then inhale slowly and deeply ... 1 - 2 - 3 - 4 ... pause. Repeat 15 times;

d. Notice how you feel after taking each Breathing Break. What do you notice? How is this different from how you felt before you started the breathing exercise?

c. If you feel that you are not as de-stressed and relaxed as you would wish, just take 15 more slow, deep breaths.

e. Set an alarm to ring hourly during your waking hours; use this as a reminder to take your Breathing Break each hour. When the alarm rings, it is important to begin your breathing cycle right away and not tell yourself that you'll do it later. When you do the Breathing Break right away, you make certain that you will get it done and not forget.

## 4. Positive Thinking:
### Positive Thinking Basics -- Brain-Science Findings:
a. Pay attention to thoughts. Thoughts are real things. They create connections – neural networks – in your brain. These neural networks form beliefs. Beliefs control actions.

If thought patterns are negative, they will literally create negative neuron patterns that fire the most (negative beliefs) and create negative reality. Similarly, if thought patterns are positive, they literally create positive neuron patterns that fire the most (positive beliefs) and create positive reality. Keep those thoughts – neuron patterns – and resultant reality positive!

b. **Positive Thinking Basics:  Eliminate Negativity –** Thought stoppage
1. Begin by noticing your thoughts
2. If your thought is positive, give yourself a huge reinforcing pat on the back

3. If you notice that you're thinking negatively, firmly tell yourself, "STOP IT!" and change the thought to a positive one
4. Build this habit to be aware of your thoughts all the time

c. **Positive Thinking Basics: Affirmation Exercises**
   1. Choose periods each day to repeat your Affirmations.
   2. Schedule these times in your planner for your Affirmation Exercises; choose the same time each day.
   3. Write out your affirmations for Good Health
   4. State your affirmations in a positive way, in the present tense and in the singular person – I, my or me
   5. At your allotted time, repeat your selected affirmations over and over in cycles of 10; state each cycle with awareness, mindfulness, and conviction
   6. Repetition allows the positive ideas to become firmly entrenched in your subconscious conscious mind ... ideas that your mind to creates
   7. For more information on how to create "Affirmations that Work!", visit **http://askdrmarlene.com/affirm.html**

d. **Positive Thinking Basics: P.M.A. – Positive Mental Attitude**

According to Edgar Cayce's prescribed remedies, cultivating a mental attitude conducive to healing was essential! Cayce believed that positive thinking prevented further consequences from emotional stress and opened the body mind to the Source of all healing – that which is spiritual and creative in nature.

He reminded those seeking physical relief that the "mind is the builder" of health as well as of illness. He described it as a demonstration of faith, for instance, to be "consistent and persistent" with treatments.

C. Resources:
  1. Professional Assistance:  Gather You Team!
    a.  Select a **Reputable Hypnotherapist**:
    When you make contact, tell the therapist what you want to accomplish – namely, the steps I've identified below. Make sure that the therapist that you have chosen has expertise in these areas.  Check that the professional you've selected has appropriate licensure and/or certification, plus membership in professional organizations, and solid experience.
    (1) Use Hypnotherapy to identify -- and remove – whatever might be blocking your Good Health and your freedom from disease;
    (2) Use Hypnotherapy to implant suggestions and techniques for effective pain relief;
    (3) Use Hypnotherapy to identify any additional steps that are required for your body to completely heal itself
    (4) Learn Self-Hypnosis
        (a).  Use **Self-Hypnosis** several times a day for pain relief
        (b).  Use **Self-Hypnosis** several times a day for relaxation and to begin conditioning your body to release illness and return to Good Health

b. Select a **Reputable Life Coach**:
When you make contact, tell the therapist what you want to accomplish – namely, the steps I've identified below. Make sure that the therapist that you have chosen has expertise in these areas. Check that the professional you've selected has appropriate licensure and/or certification, plus membership in professional organizations, and solid experience.
(1) Use **Life Coaching** to work on positive thinking, and self-care;
(2) Use **Life Coaching** to deepen self-esteem and self-acceptance, and to help you create practices to enhance these characteristics;
(3) Use **Life Coaching** to help strengthen motivation and solid commitment to your success.

c. Locate an **Experienced Naturopathic Physician** –
Again, when you make contact, check on the Physician's credentials. Once you are satisfied with the provider's expertise, schedule an appointment for a hair analysis and find out the specific supplementation your body requires for its healing
-- If your doctor advises it, get substantial **Vitamin-Mineral Supplementation** and take it consistently

d. Consult a **Qualified Medical Doctor or Physician** who understands the Cayce Remedies: begin the **Edgar Cayce Protocol** as prescribed by this Physician.

e. Choose a **Qualified Chiropractor, Osteopathic or Naturopathic Physician**.
When you make contact, tell the doctor what you want to accomplish – namely, the steps that are identified below.

Make certain that the doctor that you have chosen has expertise in these areas. Check that the professional whom you've selected has appropriate credentials, membership in professional organizations and solid experience.

-- Under the supervision of your Chiropractor, begin **Manipulation Treatment** --
    a. Use spinal manipulation to manually manipulate the vertebrae of your spinal column
    b. Use spinal manipulation to facilitate natural adjustment by breaking up congested areas
    c. Use spinal manipulation to help ganglia under strain to adjust to facilitate proper drainage
    d. Use spinal manipulation to stimulate circulation to the organs

2. Go to the A.R.E./Edgar Cayce websites:
   - **http://www.cayce.com/**
   - **http://www.edgarcayce.org/**
   Enjoy!

    a. Research the wide-variety of information available on "The Prophet" (as Edgar Cayce has been called)
    b. Research the information on Cayce's suggested remedies
    c. Purchase supplies, products, books, etc.
    d. One of the most frequently mentioned concepts in the Edgar Cayce materials is his fundamental belief that Spirit is the Life, Mind is the Builder, and the Physical is the Result.

D.  Add to your Daily Program:
     Incorporate **Diet Recommendations**

Edgar Cayce frequently emphasized the importance of maintaining a proper acid-alkaline balance by eating mostly alkaline forming foods.  According to the Cayce-recommendations, a typical diet for arthritic individuals placed emphasis on alkaline-forming foods (with 80% of the daily diet being comprised of these foods):

   * All kinds of raw vegetables except tomatoes, cabbage, dried beans, lentils, asparagus tips, and garbanzos; these may be eaten with Knox gelatin (Gelatin is seen as a catalyst in the body, helping it make use of the vitamins and other properties of vegetables and fruits)
   * All fresh fruits except strawberries, apples, cranberries, plums, olives, prunes, and blueberries (preserves and canned fruits are usually acid-forming)
   * Whole grains – pumpernickel, rye, whole wheat, black bread
   * Almonds (especially), chestnuts, Brazil nuts, & hazelnuts
   * Light proteins – fish and seafood, fowl, lamb, wild game, and liver
   * Vegetable juices, citrus fruit juices at times when cereal is not eaten.
   * Cooked leafy vegetables (except cabbage); oyster plant (salsify); parsnips; potato peelings from the baked potato, but not the potato itself.

Foods to be avoided were
   -- white flour and its products; white potatoes (except skins)
   -- fried foods
   -- carbonated drinks and alcohol
   -- fruits – apples, bananas, strawberries, tomatoes
   -- red meat (beef or veal)

Combinations of foods to be avoided were
  -- starches and sugar at the same meal
  -- coffee or tea with milk or cream, and
  -- citrus fruits or juices with cereals or dairy products

Remember Edgar Cayce's **"Attitudes & Emotions for Eating"**: if one eats in a negative frame of mind, even the most-healthy, nutritious foods can turn to poison in the system. Cayce advised to never eat when worried, angry, or extremely tired.


E. Would you like to add something really powerful? If you would like to energize your Healing activities even more fully, more effectively, there is one additional practice that I would like to suggest. I did not use this practice myself … for one very simple reason.

I did not use this practice because I did not know about it. Had I been introduced to this practice before 1980, there is absolutely no doubt that I would have used it on a daily basis as an adjunct to my own healing from arthritis. As it stands, I now use it daily to maintain my good health and healing.

Having found this to be such a profound and powerful instrument, I want to introduce you to it now. This technique is called Reiki.

Reiki is a form of energy healing, whereby Universal Energy – ki – is directed to your body for the express purpose of creating balance and good health. There are people who are trained as Reiki practitioners, who can do the treatments for you. A treatment lasts approximately an hour. After a Reiki session, you feel deeply relaxed, mentally sharp and emotionally calm.

Or, you can be trained as a Reiki practitioner and use the treatment on yourself. I strongly encourage you to consider the latter approach.

Not only is Reiki powerful for restoring and maintaining good health, but also it provides a state of deep rest and promotes an atmosphere of self-care. These are important to successful relief of dis-stress and to assist your body in its healing task.

# DAILY STEPS ON MY JOURNEY TO HEALING

## ~~ JOURNAL RECORD ~~

# DAILY STEPS ON MY JOURNEY TO HEALING
## Sunday:  Date - _____

Track the Daily Activities that Energize Your Healing Today:

|  | 8:00-<br>11:00 | 11:01-<br>2:00 | 2:01-<br>5:00 | 5:01-<br>8:00 |
|---|---|---|---|---|
| **Exercise** | | | | |
| **Meditation** | | | | |
| **Relax/Rest Breaks** | | | | |
| **Positive Thinking** | | | | |
| -- Attention to Thought | | | | |
| -- Stop Negative | | | | |
| -- Affirmations | | | | |
| -- PMA | | | | |
| **Self Hypnosis** | | | | |
| **Edgar Cayce Protocol** | | | | |
| -- Castor Oil Pack | | | | |
| -- Joint Massage | | | | |
| -- a.m. | | | | |
| -- p.m. | | | | |
| -- Atomidine | | | | |
| -- Epsom Salt Bath | | | | |
| -- Body Massage | | | | |
| -- Healthy Eating | | | | |
| -- Meal #1 | | | | |
| -- Meal #2 | | | | |
| -- Meal #3 | | | | |
| **Journal => Emotional Release** | | | | |
| **Professional Appointments** | | | | |
| -- M.D. or D.O. | | | | |
| -- Chiropractor | | | | |
| -- Naturopath | | | | |
| -- Hypnotherapist | | | | |
| -- Life Coach | | | | |
| -- Reiki Practitioner | | | | |
| -- Other: | | | | |

# DAILY STEPS ON MY JOURNEY TO HEALING
## Monday:  Date - _____

Track the Daily Activities that Energize Your Healing Today:

|  | 8:00-<br>11:00 | 11:01-<br>2:00 | 2:01-<br>5:00 | 5:01-<br>8:00 |
|---|---|---|---|---|
| **Exercise** | | | | |
| **Meditation** | | | | |
| **Relax/Rest Breaks** | | | | |
| **Positive Thinking** | | | | |
| -- Attention to Thought | | | | |
| -- Stop Negative | | | | |
| -- Affirmations | | | | |
| -- PMA | | | | |
| **Self Hypnosis** | | | | |
| **Edgar Cayce Protocol** | | | | |
| -- Castor Oil Pack | | | | |
| -- Joint Massage | | | | |
| -- a.m. | | | | |
| -- p.m. | | | | |
| -- Atomidine | | | | |
| -- Epsom Salt Bath | | | | |
| -- Body Massage | | | | |
| -- Healthy Eating | | | | |
| -- Meal #1 | | | | |
| -- Meal #2 | | | | |
| -- Meal #3 | | | | |
| **Journal => Emotional Release** | | | | |
| **Professional Appointments** | | | | |
| -- M.D. or D.O. | | | | |
| -- Chiropractor | | | | |
| -- Naturopath | | | | |
| -- Hypnotherapist | | | | |
| -- Life Coach | | | | |
| -- Reiki Practitioner | | | | |
| -- Other: | | | | |

# DAILY STEPS ON MY JOURNEY TO HEALING
## Tuesday:  Date - _____

Track the Daily Activities that Energize Your Healing Today:

|  | 8:00-11:00 | 11:01-2:00 | 2:01-5:00 | 5:01-8:00 |
|---|---|---|---|---|
| **Exercise** | | | | |
| **Meditation** | | | | |
| **Relax/Rest Breaks** | | | | |
| **Positive Thinking** | | | | |
| -- Attention to Thought | | | | |
| -- Stop Negative | | | | |
| -- Affirmations | | | | |
| -- PMA | | | | |
| **Self Hypnosis** | | | | |
| **Edgar Cayce Protocol** | | | | |
| -- Castor Oil Pack | | | | |
| -- Joint Massage | | | | |
| -- a.m. | | | | |
| -- p.m. | | | | |
| -- Atomidine | | | | |
| -- Epsom Salt Bath | | | | |
| -- Body Massage | | | | |
| -- Healthy Eating | | | | |
| -- Meal #1 | | | | |
| -- Meal #2 | | | | |
| -- Meal #3 | | | | |
| **Journal => Emotional Release** | | | | |
| **Professional Appointments** | | | | |
| -- M.D. or D.O. | | | | |
| -- Chiropractor | | | | |
| -- Naturopath | | | | |
| -- Hypnotherapist | | | | |
| -- Life Coach | | | | |
| -- Reiki Practitioner | | | | |
| -- Other: | | | | |

# DAILY STEPS ON MY JOURNEY TO HEALING
## Wednesday:  Date - _____

Track the Daily Activities that Energize Your Healing Today:

|  | 8:00-11:00 | 11:01-2:00 | 2:01-5:00 | 5:01-8:00 |
|---|---|---|---|---|
| **Exercise** | | | | |
| **Meditation** | | | | |
| **Relax/Rest Breaks** | | | | |
| **Positive Thinking** | | | | |
| -- Attention to Thought | | | | |
| -- Stop Negative | | | | |
| -- Affirmations | | | | |
| -- PMA | | | | |
| **Self Hypnosis** | | | | |
| **Edgar Cayce Protocol** | | | | |
| -- Castor Oil Pack | | | | |
| -- Joint Massage | | | | |
| -- a.m. | | | | |
| -- p.m. | | | | |
| -- Atomidine | | | | |
| -- Epsom Salt Bath | | | | |
| -- Body Massage | | | | |
| -- Healthy Eating | | | | |
| -- Meal #1 | | | | |
| -- Meal #2 | | | | |
| -- Meal #3 | | | | |
| **Journal => Emotional Release** | | | | |
| **Professional Appointments** | | | | |
| -- M.D. or D.O. | | | | |
| -- Chiropractor | | | | |
| -- Naturopath | | | | |
| -- Hypnotherapist | | | | |
| -- Life Coach | | | | |
| -- Reiki Practitioner | | | | |
| -- Other: | | | | |

# DAILY STEPS ON MY JOURNEY TO HEALING
## Thursday: Date - _____

Track the Daily Activities that Energize Your Healing Today:

| | 8:00-11:00 | 11:01-2:00 | 2:01-5:00 | 5:01-8:00 |
|---|---|---|---|---|
| **Exercise** | | | | |
| **Meditation** | | | | |
| **Relax/Rest Breaks** | | | | |
| **Positive Thinking** | | | | |
| -- Attention to Thought | | | | |
| -- Stop Negative | | | | |
| -- Affirmations | | | | |
| -- PMA | | | | |
| **Self Hypnosis** | | | | |
| **Edgar Cayce Protocol** | | | | |
| -- Castor Oil Pack | | | | |
| -- Joint Massage | | | | |
| -- a.m. | | | | |
| -- p.m. | | | | |
| -- Atomidine | | | | |
| -- Epsom Salt Bath | | | | |
| -- Body Massage | | | | |
| -- Healthy Eating | | | | |
| -- Meal #1 | | | | |
| -- Meal #2 | | | | |
| -- Meal #3 | | | | |
| **Journal => Emotional Release** | | | | |
| **Professional Appointments** | | | | |
| -- M.D. or D.O. | | | | |
| -- Chiropractor | | | | |
| -- Naturopath | | | | |
| -- Hypnotherapist | | | | |
| -- Life Coach | | | | |
| -- Reiki Practitioner | | | | |
| -- Other: | | | | |

142

# DAILY STEPS ON MY JOURNEY TO HEALING
## Friday:  Date - _____

Track the Daily Activities that Energize Your Healing Today:

|  | 8:00-11:00 | 11:01-2:00 | 2:01-5:00 | 5:01-8:00 |
|---|---|---|---|---|
| **Exercise** | | | | |
| **Meditation** | | | | |
| **Relax/Rest Breaks** | | | | |
| **Positive Thinking** | | | | |
| -- Attention to Thought | | | | |
| -- Stop Negative | | | | |
| -- Affirmations | | | | |
| -- PMA | | | | |
| **Self Hypnosis** | | | | |
| **Edgar Cayce Protocol** | | | | |
| -- Castor Oil Pack | | | | |
| -- Joint Massage | | | | |
| -- a.m. | | | | |
| -- p.m. | | | | |
| -- Atomidine | | | | |
| -- Epsom Salt Bath | | | | |
| -- Body Massage | | | | |
| -- Healthy Eating | | | | |
| -- Meal #1 | | | | |
| -- Meal #2 | | | | |
| -- Meal #3 | | | | |
| **Journal => Emotional Release** | | | | |
| **Professional Appointments** | | | | |
| -- M.D. or D.O. | | | | |
| -- Chiropractor | | | | |
| -- Naturopath | | | | |
| -- Hypnotherapist | | | | |
| -- Life Coach | | | | |
| -- Reiki Practitioner | | | | |
| -- Other: | | | | |

# DAILY STEPS ON MY JOURNEY TO HEALING
## Saturday:  Date - _____

Track the Daily Activities that Energize Your Healing Today:

|  | 8:00-11:00 | 11:01-2:00 | 2:01-5:00 | 5:01-8:00 |
|---|---|---|---|---|
| **Exercise** | | | | |
| **Meditation** | | | | |
| **Relax/Rest Breaks** | | | | |
| **Positive Thinking** | | | | |
| -- Attention to Thought | | | | |
| -- Stop Negative | | | | |
| -- Affirmations | | | | |
| -- PMA | | | | |
| **Self Hypnosis** | | | | |
| **Edgar Cayce Protocol** | | | | |
| -- Castor Oil Pack | | | | |
| -- Joint Massage | | | | |
| -- a.m. | | | | |
| -- p.m. | | | | |
| -- Atomidine | | | | |
| -- Epsom Salt Bath | | | | |
| -- Body Massage | | | | |
| -- Healthy Eating | | | | |
| -- Meal #1 | | | | |
| -- Meal #2 | | | | |
| -- Meal #3 | | | | |
| **Journal => Emotional Release** | | | | |
| **Professional Appointments** | | | | |
| -- M.D. or D.O. | | | | |
| -- Chiropractor | | | | |
| -- Naturopath | | | | |
| -- Hypnotherapist | | | | |
| -- Life Coach | | | | |
| -- Reiki Practitioner | | | | |
| -- Other: | | | | |

144

*By accepting yourself fully, exactly the way*

*you are right now, you become free to change.*

-- Dr. Anna Wayne

Greetings,

This is Dr. Marlene Shiple, the Life Coach Dr. I want to thank you sincerely for your interest in *Arthritis Pain … FREE!: Heal Arthritis Naturally – I Did, You Can, Too!* I hope you are finding it intriguing, usable, *and* informative!

In addition, it is my fond hope that you treated yourself to completing the "JOURNEY TO HEALING Journal Record" on the previous pages. Investing your energy in this undertaking – and doing so FOR YOURSELF – can speed up your progress toward creating the Life – the Reality – of your Dreams!

If you are reading this and have not yet completed the "Journal Record" section, I invite you to go back and do so now! I assure you that it takes only a brief amount of time each day! In return for you investing your time and energy in this way, I give you the following assurance: What you invest to create changes in Your Life, earns you <u>massive</u> benefits. These benefits are in direct proportion to your investment. By making this investment, YOU – and **you** alone – are the A-#1, All-time WINNER!

I encourage you to invest for the WIN. YOU **are** worth it!!

Warm regards,

*Marlene Shiple, Ph.D*
The Life Coach Dr.

146

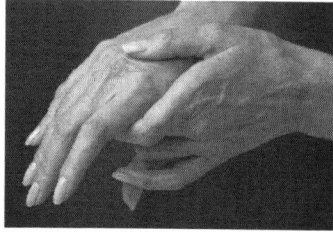

To view our Extensive selection of
Hypnosis-CD/Workbook Programs and
Meditation CD Recordings, kindly visit us at
**http://thelifecoachdr.com/coach**
and click on Coaching Products (All)

**Marlene Shiple, Ph.D.
The Life Coach Dr.
http://thelifecoachdr.com/coach
(602) 266 – 6662**

To learn more about Life Coaching and
to view our Hypnosis videos and Hypnosis-CD-
plus-Workbook Programs, come by today
for a visit at **http://thelifecoachdr.com/coach**

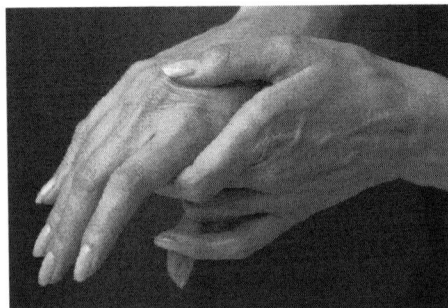

**Marlene Shiple, Ph.D.**
**The Life Coach Dr.**
**http://thelifecoachdr.com/coach**
**(602) 266 – 6662**